WARTIME MISSIONS OF HARRY L. HOPKINS

WARTIME MISSIONS

OF HARRY L. HOPKINS

MATTHEW B. WILLS

PENTLAND PRESS, INC.
ENGLAND•USA•SCOTLAND

PUBLISHED BY PENTLAND PRESS, INC.
5124 Bur Oak Circle, Raleigh, North Carolina 27612
United States of America
919-782-0281

ISBN 1-57197-012-6
Library of Congress Catalog Card Number 95-072729

Printed in the United States of America

To

JULIA RYAN WILLS

TABLE OF CONTENTS

Foreword

So much has been written about the remarkable accomplishments of Harry Lloyd Hopkins in resolving the two greatest challenges of this nation during the 20th century, the Great Depression and World War II, that it is appropriate to record those aspects of his early life which prepared him for the tasks for which he is known.

Born in Sioux City, Iowa, in 1890, his family moved eastward to Grinnell, where Harry attended grammar school, high school and, in 1912, Grinnell College. The family was of modest means. His father, David A. Hopkins, was a harness maker who had ample time for other activities since the advent of the automobile sharply reduced the need for his trade. A happy-go-lucky man, he devoted most of his time to bowling to the distress of his wife, Anna, a rather stern, strong woman who was a pillar of the Methodist Church. She instilled in Harry a strong sense of social justice, while his father gave him the zest for the lighter side of life.

At Grinnell College, Harry was an average student, more remembered for his prowess on the basketball court than for his academic performance. He did, however, have a lively interest in college politics. During his summer vacations, he worked in a local brickyard, which gave him an understanding of hard, manual labor. Perhaps the most enduring contribution Grinnell College bestowed on him was a sense of responsibility toward the impoverished, people who through no fault of their own, found themselves pulled down by crop failures or other disasters. One of his professors, Dr. Edward Steiner, was particularly influential in reinforcing his sense of social ethics. It was Dr. Steiner who, when Harry graduated from Grinnell College, gave him the lead to Christadora House in New York City, a charitable organization devoted to improving the condition of slum families in New York's lower east side.

He got a job at Christadora House Summer Camp as a counselor in Bound Brook, New Jersey, where children of poor families were sent to get out of the city into the fresh air of the country. Here, Harry was exposed to the children of the grinding poverty of the city, the kind of economic desperation unknown in the Midwest. The missionary zeal of his mother welled up in him and he became determined to become the champion of the poor. At the end of summer he went to work at Christadora House itself. He was paid five dollars a month plus room and board. It was at Christadora House that he met a fellow social worker, Ethel Gross. They fell in love and were married, bound by their mutual attraction and their goal of improving the lot of the poor.

It was in New York City that he met Dr. John Kingsbury, the director of the Association for Improving the Condition of the Poor

(AICP), a man who was to have a great influence on his life and his career. He became Harry's mentor and good friend. He gave him a job at the AICP at $40 a month. Harry held down both jobs, at Christadora House by day and at the AICP by night. At the AICP he was trained and put in charge of an emergency employment bureau in the waterfront, the roughest section of New York's slums.

Impressed by his performance, John Kingsbury, by then Commissioner of Public Charities, recommended him for the job of executive secretary of the New York Board of Child Welfare, at a salary of $3,000 a year. He was twenty-three years old.

When the United States entered World War I in 1917, he tried to enlist, but was rejected because he was virtually blind in one eye. He then joined the Red Cross and was appointed director of the Gulf Division. He later was promoted to director of all Red Cross activities for the Southeastern states. Here he was primarily concerned with providing aid to widows and orphans of soldiers who died in that conflict. When the Mississippi flooded over its banks, he led the relief effort to help those who lost their homes and belongings in the flood.

At the end of the war John Kingsbury again took him in hand and appointed him director of the AICP, Division of Health, at $8,000 a year, a job he held for six years. In 1924, while maintaining his association with the AICP, he moved on to become director of the New York Tuberculosis Association. Here too, his leadership led to important changes and improvements. He merged the New York Tuberculosis Association with the New York Heart Association, thus broadening its range of activities. He changed the name to New York Tuberculosis and Health Association. He then added the Children's Welfare Federation, the Allied Dental Clinic and the Associated Out-Patient Clinic. To finance its expanded operations he established the Christmas and Easter Seal program. When he learned that workers drilling the rock under the city were being stricken with silicosis, he had a study prepared which led to the invention of a vacuum device which extracted silica dust from the workplace.

With the stock market crash and ensuing unemployment crisis he raised funds from the Red Cross to put unemployed men to work on park projects. He worked at night at the AICP assigning jobs to the destitute.

When Franklin D. Roosevelt was elected governor of New York and he established a work relief program called the Temporary Emergency Relief Administration (TERA) to deal with the unemployment crisis in New York State, the name of Harry Hopkins was brought to his attention. Governor Roosevelt appointed him chairman of the TERA. In view of the temporary nature of this assignment, Harry held onto his job as director of New York Tuberculosis and Health Association. At the TERA he administered a fund of $30 million to put men to work at useful jobs, in contrast to President Hoover's policy of simply doling out money to the unemployed. It soon became evident that the TERA was not temporary at all, but would go on for several years. So Harry resigned from his position at New York Tuberculosis and Health Association, taking a sharp decrease in salary, to devote his full attention to the TERA.

The TERA became a model for Roosevelt when he was elected president in 1932. He asked Harry Hopkins to come down to Washington for two weeks to draft out a national work relief program. During President Roosevelt's first one hundred days he appointed Harry Hopkins Federal Emergency Relief Administrator. The TERA went through several transformations, emerging finally as the Works Progress Administration (WPA), which Harry Hopkins administered at an annual salary of $8,000, a dramatic drop from his $15,000 annual salary at New York Tuberculosis and Health Association.

At the outset the president instructed Hopkins to find jobs for four million men and women in thirty days, and he accomplished this feat. In the course of his administration of work relief, Hopkins spent nine billion dollars of public funds and provided tens of millions of Americans with gainful employment. The projects they built—schools, libraries, public buildings, highways, airports, bridges and dams—strengthened America beyond measure. In addition the WPA provided jobs to people according to their abilities and talents. Writers produced the American Guide Series, the best guidebooks ever written about the American states and cities; actors, producers, stagehands, musicians and directors produced plays in previously darkened theaters and established traveling companies to bring the living theater to every city, town and hamlet in America. At least as important, the WPA restored a sense of self-respect in the minds and hearts of desperate men and women.

This, then, was the background and professional formation of the man described in Matthew Wills' *Wartime Missions of Harry L. Hopkins*, a man who, I am proud to say, was my father.

Robert Hopkins
Washington, D.C.

ACKNOWLEDGEMENTS

I first met Robert Hopkins on a warm May morning in 1993 at the Lauinger Library of Georgetown University. From that day onward I have been the recipient of his kindness and consideration regarding my efforts to write of his father's wartime missions. I will always be grateful to him.

Robert asked his friend, Arthur Schlesinger Jr., to read Part I of my manuscript. Not only did he do so, but he generously shared his thoughts for improving and expanding it. He wrote me, "also you will want to add something about Churchill, Hopkins, and the Soviet Union." That suggestion led me to write of Hopkins' first mission to Russia. I wish to express my deep appreciation to Professor Schlesinger.

I would be remiss not to mention two other distinguished academics, Dr. Lloyd E. Worner, president emeritus of Colorado College and Gene R. Nichol, the former dean of the University of Colorado School of Law. Dr. Worner's words of encouragement have meant more to me than I can say. Gene Nichol, whose love of history is only exceeded by his love of the law, has given me his steadfast support. I thank him for that and for all of the good conversations we have had.

Over fifty-four years ago Flight Lieutenant David C. McKinley, D.F.C. of the Royal Air Force flew Harry Hopkins to Russia through hostile skies on a flight of over twenty hours. He is now a retired air vice marshal living on Alderney in the Channel Islands. I have sent him far too many questions to which he has always responded with graciousness and care. I appreciate his invaluable assistance.

After I completed Part I, which focuses on Hopkins' January 1941 mission to meet Churchill, I sent it to Richard M. Langworth, president of the International Churchill Society of the United States with a request that he forward it to The Lady Soames, D.B.E. In due course I received her handwritten reply in which she wrote, "I have read your manuscript with enormous interest and not a little emotion." I cherish her letter.

I thank Nicholas B. Scheetz, manuscripts librarian of Special Collections at the Lauinger Library of Georgetown University, Robert Parks, archivist at the Franklin D. Roosevelt Library, Marti Gansz, assistant to the archivist/librarian at the George C. Marshall Research Foundation, Samuel W. Rushay, archivist at the Harry S. Truman Library and Alan Williams of the Imperial War Museum for their uncommon courtesy.

I wish to express my deep appreciation to our children for their encouragement.

This book is dedicated to my wife. I have done so out of devotion and out of my knowledge that she possesses a quality which Harry Hopkins had in abundance. It is called courage.

Sculpture of Harry L. Hopkins by Jo Davidson. Courtesy of Grinnell College.

PART I

CHURCHILL AND HOPKINS

When Winston Churchill and Harry Hopkins first met, the British leader had only recently come through what his daughter, Lady Soames, has called "those great and hard times." For those born after the Second World War, "those great and hard times" may seem too dim and distant to appreciate. Some knowledge of these events, however, is essential to any understanding of their relationship.

On May 10, 1940, hours before Churchill assumed his duties as prime minister, Hitler unleashed a blitzkrieg against Holland, Belgium, and Luxembourg. Within four days German armor had broken the French line at Sedan. By May 20, German panzer divisions had driven a wedge at least twenty miles wide from the Ardennes to the Channel cutting off the British Expeditionary Force (BEF) from the French Army. On May 28, without warning, King Leopold surrendered the Belgian Army. The BEF was saved from almost certain destruction by a hastily organized evacuation from the port of Dunkirk. All of their heavy equipment and most of their light arms were abandoned in France. On June 10, 1940, Italy entered the war on Germany's side. Churchill had hoped to convince the French leaders to continue the war from their colonies in North Africa; however, on June 17 the French cabinet asked the German government for terms.

His country stood alone and Churchill was faced with the greatest challenge of his life. Many thought that England was finished. Among them was the outspoken United States ambassador to Great Britain, Joseph P. Kennedy. On August 2, 1940, Kennedy cabled the president a message indicating that if the Germans possessed the air power that they claimed, the RAF (Royal Air Force) would be eliminated following which a British surrender "would be inevitable." [1] When the Luftwaffe was unable to defeat the Royal Air Force in August and early September, Hitler decided to break the morale of the British people by bombing civilian targets. After the first largescale attack on London on September 7, Kennedy told his friend Harvey Klemmer that "the British have had it. They can't stop the Germans and the best thing for them is to learn to live with them." [2]

In the middle of October Kennedy was abruptly recalled, never to return as ambassador. At a press conference in the U.S. Kennedy asserted, "I never made anti-Britsh statements or said, on or off the record, that I do not expect Britain to win the war." [3] A few weeks later Kennedy met with Charles and Anne Lindbergh at his suite in the Waldorf Tower. Lindbergh's diary for November 29 revealed Kennedy's real views on the war:

> He feels as we do, that the British position is hopeless and that the best possible thing for them would be a negotiated peace in the near future...He said the war would stop if it were not for Churchill and the hope in England that America will come in. [4]

With Kennedy's departure a new chapter in Anglo-American relations was about to unfold. After the failure of the Sumner Welles mission in early 1940, Roosevelt never openly sent a high-ranking official to Britain other than Kennedy. Following his reelection in November, Roosevelt felt far less constrained by political considerations. On January 5, 1941, he announced at a press conference that Mr. Harry L. Hopkins would be going to England as his personal representative. In some ways Hopkins was an odd choice. He had no experience in diplomacy. Directing the Federal Emergency Relief Organization and the Works Progress Administration during Roosevelt's First Administration had been his crowning achievements. He had become a favorite of the President who liked "his quickness, his sympathy, and his unique mixture of cynicism and idealism." [5]

Although Hopkins was only fifty, his health was precarious. In 1937 he had a large portion of his stomach removed on account of cancer. Although there was never any recurrence of his cancer, his operation left him vulnerable to serious nutritional deficiencies. On September 8, 1939, he wrote his brother, Lewis:

> I am not absorbing proteins or fats in any adequate means. My protein count, or whatever you call it, is one-third normal...I have had a very serious edema in my feet which is fairly well cleared up. My eyesight is going back on me, and I have lost about thirty pounds from my top weight about a year ago. I weigh about 130 pounds now. [6]

Shortly after this letter Roosevelt told friends, "The doctors have given Harry up for dead." [7] Nevertheless, after extensive treatment at the Mayo Clinic and at a Navy hospital in Washington, his condition slowly improved. Despite ill health and inexperience, Hopkins had one incomparable factor in his favor: Roosevelt trusted him implicitly. The start of Hopkins' mission was inauspicious. He was five days en route. The Neutrality Law prevented a direct flight to England. After flying to Lisbon on the Pan American clipper, he took a British Overseas Airways clipper to Poole on the south coast of England. Churchill had directed one of his closest associates, his parliamentary private secretary, Brendan Bracken, to meet Hopkins' airplane and to escort him to London. When the passengers disembarked, Hopkins was nowhere to be seen. Bracken found him on the plane appearing sick and shrunken, too exhausted to get out of his seat. Hopkins arrived at Waterloo station in London just after 7:00 P.M. Thursday, January 9. Minutes after his arrival incendiary bombs showered down between Clapham Junction and Waterloo which closed the line for hours.

Churchill had invited him to dine at No. 10 Downing Street that first evening, but as he was too tired to face Churchill, he dined in his room at Claridge's Hotel with Herschel V. Johnson, charge d'affaires of the American Embassy. The first meeting with Churchill took place over lunch the next day. Hopkins described the scene to Roosevelt as follows:

> *Bracken led me to a little dining room in the basement, poured me some sherry and left me to wait for the Prime Minister. A rotund—smiling—redfaced gentleman appeared—extended a fat but nevertheless convincing hand and wished me welcome to England. A short black coat—striped trousers—a clear eye and a mushy voice was the impression of England's leader as he showed me with obvious pride the photograph of his beautiful daughter-in-law and grandchild.* [8]

Later in their conversation Hopkins bluntly spoke what was on his mind. He told Churchill there was a feeling in some quarters that Churchill did not like America, Americans, or Roosevelt. Hopkins wrote to the president, "This set him off on a bitter tho [*sic*] fairly constrained attack on Ambassador Kennedy who he believes is responsible for this impression." [9] Despite Hopkins' bluntness their initial meeting was so warm and cordial that it lasted most of the afternoon. The youngest of Churchill's private secretaries, 26-year-old John Colville, recorded in his diary:

*The President's envoy, Mr. Hopkins, was lunching with
the P.M. and they were so impressed with each other that
their tête-à-tête did not break up till nearly 4:00. Then we
left for Ditchley, I travelling down with Brendan. Brendan
said that Hopkins, the confidant of Roosevelt, was the most
important American visitor to this country we had ever
had.* [10]

Ditchley, near Woodstock north of Oxford, was an exception-
ally beautiful seventeenth century home then owned by Ronald
and Nancy Tree. Ronald Tree, the grandson of the original
Marshall Fields, had placed his estate at the disposal of the
prime minister. Churchill invited Hopkins to spend his first
weekend in England at Ditchley. Their first evening is described
in Colville's diary. "Dinner at Ditchley takes place in a magnifi-
cent setting. The dining room is lit only by candles, in a large
chandelier and on the walls. The table is not overdecorated:
four gilt candle sticks with tall yellow tapers and a single gilt
culp in the centre." [11] Among the weekend guests were Venetia
Montagu, Oliver Lyttelton, Freda Casa Maury, and Professor
Lindemann. Hopkins, who knew none of the other guests, was
the center of attention. Colville recounted the following dialogue
between Hopkins and Churchill:

*When the ladies had gone, Mr. Hopkins paid a graceful
tribute to the P.M.'s, speeches which had, he said, produced the most stirring and revolutionary effect on all
classes and districts in America. At an American Cabinet
meeting the President had had a wireless set brought in so
that all might listen to the Prime Minister. The P.M. was
touched and gratified. He said that he hardly knew what
he said in his speeches last summer; he had just been
imbued with the feeling that "it would be better for us to be
destroyed than to see the triumph of such an imposter."
When at the time of Dunkirk, he had addressed a meeting
of Ministers "below the line" he had realized that there was
only one thing they wanted to hear him say; that whatever
happened to our army we should still go on. He had said
it.* [12]

Churchill and Hopkins spent their entire weekend at
Ditchley. For Hopkins this was a totally new experience. He
had lived at the White House as a guest of the president since
May 10, but on weekends Roosevelt eschewed social life as
much as possible and seldom stayed up as late as midnight. On
Sunday evening, while Churchill and Hopkins were watching a

film, the telephone rang and the prime minister was informed a cruiser, *Southampton*, had been destroyed by Stuka dive bombers in the Mediterranean. This marked the first appearance by the Luftwaffe in that theater. Hopkins, who had no experience with the realities of war, was amazed at the calmness of Churchill and his staff in the face of such a serious loss. Churchill then proceeded to initiate Hopkins in one of his after-dinner appreciations of the war situation.

Churchill expressed himself pacing about in front of the fire at the far end of the library from midnight till 2:00 A.M., all the while smoking a phenomenally large cigar. Hopkins was not one overly impressed by eloquence alone; however, he was nearly always influenced by those who knew their facts. That evening convinced Hopkins that Churchill had encyclopaedic knowledge of the logistics of war, as well as an incomparable command of the English language.

Throughout his stay in Britain, Hopkins kept Roosevelt fully apprised of his activities and his impressions. One of his first reports to the president followed his weekend at Ditchley. It was written in longhand on Claridge's stationery and read in part:

Dear Mr. President:

These notes are sent by Col. Lee who is returning with Halifax. Will you save them for me until I get back when I shall try to put them in readable form.

The people here are amazing from Churchill down and if courage alone can win—the result will be inevitable. But they need our help desperately and I am sure you will permit nothing to stand in the way. Some of the ministers and underlings are a bit trying but no more than some I have seen.

Churchill is the gov't in every sense of the word—he controls the grand strategy and often the details—labor trusts him—the army, navy, air force are behind him to a man. The politicians and upper crust pretend to like him. I cannot emphasize too strongly that he is the one and only person over here with whom you need to have a full meeting of minds.

Churchill wants to see you—the sooner the better—but I have told him of your problem until the bill is passed. I am convinced this meeting between you and Churchill is essential—and soon—for the battering continues and Hitler does not wait for Congress. [13]

The bill referred to was the Lend Lease Bill then pending in Congress which would provide military supplies and arms to

Churchill and Hopkins with Vice Admiral Sir Gordon Ramsay K.C.B. at a port in Northern Scotland en route to Scapa Flow.

Great Britain on a vast scale without requiring immediate payments. On Tuesday, January 14, Churchill and Hopkins left London by special train for Scotland. Their ultimate destination was Scapa Flow where Lord Halifax was departing for America to be the ambassador to the United States. The final stage of their journey was on a destroyer which they boarded with some difficulty. Churchill scrambled aboard, but Hopkins, suffering from cold and fatigue, missed his footing and nearly fell into the sea.

Scapa Flow, a large, natural anchorage surrounded by the Orkney Islands, was the operational base of the home fleet. Churchill, who was

Lord Halifax and Hopkins at a luncheon on HMS King George V on January 15, 1941.

aware of Roosevelt's interest in naval warfare, wanted Hopkins to see Britain's newest and most powerful battleship, *King*

Luncheon on King George V on January 15, 1941 which included Prime Minister and Mrs. Churchill, Lord and Lady Halifax, Hopkins, Capt. Patterson and Cmdr. C. R. (Tommy) Thompson, Churchill's A.D.C.

With permission of the Imperial War Museum

George V. On January 15, Churchill arranged an inspection of this warship with a luncheon on board for Lord and Lady Halifax at which Hopkins sat between Lord Halifax and Captain Patterson, the ship's captain. That night Churchill and Hopkins were the guests of honor at a dinner on HMS *Nelson.* Their host was Admiral Sir John Tovey, commander in chief of the home fleet. Among the other guests were Vice Admiral Lancelot Holland, Captain Frederick Dalrymple-Hamilton, and Captain William George Tennant. Each officer was destined to be part of a momentous naval battle before

For'd Door		After Door
	The Flag Lieutenant	
Commander Thompson		Captain Agnew
Captain Gordon		Captain Graham
Paymr. Captain Grace		The Captain of the Fleet
Captain Madden		Captain Dalrymple-Hamilton
The Chief of Staff		Vice-Admiral Holland
Major General Sir H. Ismay		The Rt. Hon. Winston Spencer Churchill
The Flag Captain		The Commander -in- Chief
Rear-Admiral Hallifax		Mr. Harry Hopkins
Captain Tennant		Rear-Admiral Curteis
Captain Curzon-Howe		Captain Blackman
Captain (E) Ford		Sir Charles Wilson
Captain Arliss		Captain Dundas
Captain Chapman		Surgn. Captain Fitzroy-Williams
Mr. Seal		Captain Hughes-Hallett
	The Secretary	

Obtained from the Imperial War Museum. Found in the Harry L. Hopkins Papers, Special Collections Division, Georgetown University Library.

Dinner seating chart on board HMS Nelson on Wednesday, January 15, 1941.

the year was out. Vice Admiral Holland would perish on Hood when it blew up after being hit by shells from the *Bismarck.* Admiral Tovey would be on the bridge of *King George V* when *Rodney* and *King George V* pounded a crippled *Bismarck* to a hulk. In that same engagement Captain Dalrymple-Hamilton would command *Rodney.* When Japanese naval aircraft sank *Repulse* and the *Prince of Wales* off the coast of Malaya, Capt. Tennant would be the captain of *Repulse.*

That January night the guns were silent while Hopkins dined with a former First Lord of the Admiralty who loved the Royal Navy, its illustrious history, its proud traditions, and all those officers and men "that go down to the sea in ships." [14] Leaving Scapa, Churchill and Hopkins returned to Thurso on the north coast of Scotland in stormy seas. Their last night in Scotland was at Glasgow. Sir Charles Wilson, Churchill's personal physician, kept a diary. His entry captured an enduring moment:

With permission of the Imperial War Museum

Churchill and Hopkins on board HMS King George V at Scapa Flow on January 15, 1941.

Churchill and Hopkins visit a Fleet Air Arm Station in January 1941.

On the return journey, Tom Johnston dined us at the Station Hotel at Glasgow, and I set next to Harry Hopkins, an unkempt figure. After a time he got up and, turning to the P.M., said: "I suppose you wish to know what I am going to say to President Roosevelt on my return. Well, I'm going to quote you one verse from that Book of Books in the truth of which Mr. Johnston's mother and my own Scottish mother were brought up: 'Whither thou goest, I will go; and where thou lodgest, I will lodge; thy people shall be my people, and thy God my God.'" Then he added very quietly,

*"Even to the end." I was surprised to find the P.M. in tears.
He knew what it meant.* [15]

Churchill and Hopkins arrived back in London on Saturday, January 18, in a snowstorm. The tireless Churchill and his gritty American guest immediately departed for Chequers, the prime minister's official country residence, for the weekend. Hopkins had been in Britain for only ten days, but in that period he had met most of those closest to Churchill. Even before he had arrived at No. 10 Downing Street, he had made a courtesy call at the Foreign Office to meet Lord Halifax and Anthony Eden. At Ditchley Hopkins had met Professor Lindemann, Churchill's interpreter of all technical matters, whether scientific or economic, who was as close to Churchill as anyone outside his family. On the train from London to northern Scotland Hopkins had traveled with General Sir Hastings Ismay, universally known as Pug, who was, throughout the war, the main channel of communication between Churchill and the chiefs of staff. The guests at Chequers on Saturday, January 18, and Sunday, January 19, included Admiral of the Fleet Sir Dudley Pound, Air Marshal Sholto Douglas, as well as Ismay and Lindemann.

Churchill clearly wanted Hopkins to meet those admirals and generals who directed the war effort, but he also wanted Hopkins to know his family, especially his wife, Clementine. She had been with Hopkins at Ditchley the previous weekend. They had journeyed together to Scapa Flow. She was Hopkins' hostess his first weekend at Chequers where he also met two of the Churchill children, Randolph and Mary. Eric Seal, who was the duty private secretary at Chequers for the weekend, wrote of Hopkins, "He is really a very charming and interesting man." [16] Hopkins, too, had been charmed, especially by his hostess. After the war Robert Sherwood described Hopkins' lasting impression of Clementine Churchill, "In Hopkins' opinion, there was no doubt that the most charming and entertaining of all the people he met on those weekends was Mrs. Churchill." [17]

During his stay in Britain, Hopkins spent one weekend with Churchill at Ditchley and three weekends with him at Chequers. Of the first fourteen nights in Britain he had spent twelve of them with the prime minister. At least one memorable evening was spent without Churchill. On Wednesday, January 22, Lord Beaverbrook, the press baron and Minister of Aircraft Production, gave a dinner for Hopkins at Claridge's. The guests were newspaper editors, writers, and managers. One of them left the following account:

We were all tired men, suffering from a succession of long nights, during which London had been bombed by explosives and incendiaries, and during which the difficulties of newspaper production had been extreme. But on that midwinter evening in the peak period of the first series of London blitzes we were also intensely curious men— which is the happiest and healthiest state for a journalist in any clime or circumstance. All of us were wondering as our cars advanced cautiously through the blackout toward Claridge's...what Hopkins would have to say to us...

When the waiters had cleared the tables, the doors were closed, and Beaverbrook stood up, smiling. He addressed himself not to us, but to Harry Hopkins. For days, he said, Hopkins had been talking to members of the Government. But tonight was a yet more important occasion, for those present were "the masters of the Government" the leaders of the British Press. And so he invited Mr. Hopkins to speak to us.

Hopkins rose, looking lean, shy, and untidy, grasping the back of his chair, and he continued to look shy throughout his speech.

His words were private, so no notes were taken. But if it had been possible to record the sentences that came quietly and diffidently from the lips of Harry Hopkins, they would have compared well for nobility of expression with the splendid oration which Mr. Roosevelt had delivered two days earlier when he was sworn in for the third time as President of the United States.

Not that Hopkins repeated or even echoed the President's speech. He talked in more intimate terms. Where the President had spoken of America's duty to the world, Hopkins told us how the President and those around him were convinced that America's world duty could be successfully performed only in partnership with Britain. He told us of the anxiety and admiration with which every phase of Britain's lonely struggle was watched from the White House, and of his own emotions as he travelled through our blitzed land. His speech left us with the feeling that although America was not yet in the war, she was marching beside us, and that should we stumble she would see we did not fall. Above all, he convinced us that the President and the men about him blazed with faith in the future of Democracy. [18]

Hopkins' mission was originally intended to last only two weeks. He was enjoying himself enormously and requested Roosevelt's permission to stay on which was granted. Before Hopkins returned to Chequers in the early evening on Friday, January 24, he and Churchill visited the batteries at Dover. The previous summer, on Churchill's insistence, a 14-inch gun had been emplaced at Dover to shell German batteries and other installations across the Channel. Colville's diary does not reveal Hopkins' impression of the Dover batteries. It does disclose Hopkins' interest in the attitudes of working class people. His natural inclination was to move about freely and talk to as many people as possible; however, his busy schedule gave him little opportunity to do this. At Dover Hopkins overheard one work-man exclaim as Churchill passed by, "There goes the bloody British Empire." [19] That evening, in Colville's presence, Hopkins told Churchill what the workman had said. Colville's diary reveals Churchill's obvious delight: "Winston's face wreathed itself in smiles and, turning to me, he lisped, 'Very nice.' I don't think anything has given him such pleasure for a long time." [20]

Hopkins spent Friday, January 24, and the next two nights at Chequers. By then Churchill and Hopkins had developed a rapport that went far beyond mere friendship. Each enjoyed the other's company, but what instinctively bonded them was the mutual understanding that each man was totally committed to winning the war regardless of any personal cost. John Colville described Churchill's mood and the tenor of the conversation on Sunday evening:

> *During dinner the P.M. was very hilarious and in the same amiable frame of mind as he had been the whole weekend...When the women had gone to bed, I listened in the Great Hall to as interesting a discussion as I ever hope to hear. We sat in a circle, Portal (Air Vice Marshal Sir Charles Portal), Hopkins, Jack Churchill, myself, and Prof (Professor Frederick Lindemann), while the P.M. stood with his back against the mantlepiece, a cigar between his teeth, his hands in the armpits of his waistcoat...All the while a torrent of eloquence flowed from his lips, and he would fix one or another of us with his eye as he drove home some point. He talked of the past, the present, and the future...*
>
> *The P.M...asked Hopkins for his views. Speaking slow-ly but emphatically, Hopkins stated that the President was not much concerned with the future. His preoccupation was with the next few months...All he (Hopkins) would say*

of the future was that he believed the Anglo-Saxon peoples would have to do the rearrangement: the other nations would not be ripe for co-operation for a long time...

As far as the present was concerned, there were four divisions of public opinion in America: a small group of Nazis and Communists, sheltering behind Lindbergh, who declared for a negotiated peace and wanted a German victory; a group represented by Joe Kennedy, which said "Help Britain, but make damn sure you don't get into any danger of war"; a majority group which supported the

Hopkins, Mrs. Churchill, Churchill and the Mayor of Southampton inspecting bomb damage on January 31, 1941.

Churchill and Hopkins in Portsmouth on January 31, 1941. One whole street had ceased to exist.

With permission of the Imperial War Museum

*President's determination to send the maximum assistance
at whatever risk; and about ten percent or fifteen percent of
the country, including Knox, Stimson, and most of the
armed forces, who were in favor of immediate war.*

*The important element in the situation was the boldness
of the President, who would lead opinion and not follow it,
who was convinced that if England lost, America, too,
would be encircled and beaten.* [21]

The following weekend Hopkins spent only one night at
Chequers. Churchill had invited him to stay for the entire weekend, but Wendell Willkie, Roosevelt's recent political opponent,
had also been invited for the weekend. Hopkins felt that Willkie
would prefer to talk to Churchill alone.

On Friday Churchill took Hopkins to look at bomb damage at
Southampton and Portsmouth. In Portsmouth they saw extensive damage. On one street not a single building remained
intact. Afterwards, on Friday evening, they returned to
Chequers. From there Eric Seal, Churchill's principal private
secretary, wrote to his wife:

> *We came straight back here by special train. Hopkins
> came with us all the way and spent the night. It was quite
> a small party. P.M., Mrs. C., Hopkins, General Ismay,
> Commander Thompson (Tommy) & myself. P.M. was in
> great form. He gets on like a house afire with Hopkins,
> who is a dear & is universally liked.* [22]

One week later on Saturday, February 8, Hopkins made a
final visit to Chequers to say goodbye to the Churchill family. It
was probably his most productive time with Churchill, who was
working on a speech to be broadcast to the entire world on the
following evening. The same day the House of Representatives
had passed the Lend Lease Bill by a vote of 260 to 165. The
final decision would be up to the Senate. One of the prime
objectives of Churchill's speech was to convince America that
this bill could make the difference between victory and defeat.
Hopkins had suggestions that might appeal to the Senate and
together they worked on the final version of his speech into the
night. Late on Saturday night Hopkins left by special train for
Bournemouth accompanied by Brendan Bracken, Commander
Thompson, and Lieutenant Anthony McComas, who safeguarded
voluminous secret papers that Hopkins was taking back to
Washington. Before his departure Hopkins wrote Churchill:

My dear Mr. Prime Minister, I shall never forget these days with you—your supreme confidence and will to victory—Britain I have ever liked—I like it the more.

As I leave for America tonight I wish you great and good luck—confusion to your enemies—victory for Britain.

Ever so cordially, Harry Hopkins. [23]

On Sunday evening in the lounge of Branksome Tower Hotel, Hopkins and the others listened to Churchill's broadcast. Churchill ended his speech with these words:

We shall not fail or falter; we shall not weaken or tire. Neither the sudden shock of battle, nor the long-drawn trials of vigilance and exertion will wear us down. Give us the tools, and we will finish the job. [24]

The next day, Monday, February 10, Hopkins and Lieutenant McComas boarded the clipper for America. Their route took them to Lisbon, far down the west coast of Africa, then across the Atlantic to Brazil, and finally north to the United States. These thirty-two days in the British Isles had been a transformation for Hopkins. Before, he was a domestic political figure largely unknown outside the United States. Afterwards, he was a world class statesman who in time would become Franklin Roosevelt's closest foreign policy adviser.

What else had Hopkins' mission accomplished? There is no doubt that Hopkins had been able to reassure Roosevelt that Churchill and the British people had the will to win. Both Hopkins and Roosevelt concluded that self-interest and moral necessity required America to support Britain. On a personal level Hopkins had instilled hope in many a heart. Sir Charles Wilson, Churchill's physician, after listening to Hopkins quote from the Book of Ruth, wrote in his diary, "Even to us the words seemed like a rope thrown to a drowning man." [25] One of the editors at Lord Beaverbrook's dinner for Hopkins recalled:

Many a tragic and terrible chapter was to be added to our country's history before our prayers were answered and our efforts rewarded. None of us British journalists who had been listening to the man from the White House was in any illusion about the peril which encompassed our island. But we were happy men all; our confidence and our courage had been stimulated by a contact for which Shakespeare, in Henry V, *had a phrase: "A little touch of Harry in the night."* [26]

John Colville had seen the rapport between Churchill and Hopkins at No. 10 Downing Street, during that first weekend at Ditchley, and over a long weekend at Chequers. He, too, was affected by Hopkins. On the day of Hopkins' departure Colville wrote:

> I am confident that we have won. We shall see much serious damage and undergo many trials and dangers, but with the certainty of American help and the determination of the people, the ultimate issue cannot be in doubt. [27]

Hopkins' visit made a lasting impression on Churchill's daughter-in-law, Pamela. Long afterwards she would reflect, "Perhaps no one, who was not there, could fully appreciate the impact he made, especially on the great war leader who would become his friend." [28]

Churchill was confident of Roosevelt's support, but knew that only Congress could declare war and that unless Congress passed the Lend Lease Bill America's help would be far less than Roosevelt and Hopkins had envisioned. On Saturday night, March 8, the bill finally passed the Senate. Hopkins immediately placed a transatlantic telephone call to Churchill. That night John Colville was the duty private secretary. He took the call at 3:00 A.M. The next day Churchill cabled Hopkins, "Prime Minister to Hopkins-Thank God for your news. Strain is serious. Kindest Regards." [29] Simultaneously he cabled Roosevelt, "To President Roosevelt from Former Naval Person—Our blessings from the whole British Empire go out to you and the American Nation for this very present help in time of trouble." [30]

For Churchill Hopkins' visit had been a harbinger of the Lend Lease Bill which guaranteed the means of Britain's survival, but it represented much more. The spirit of Hopkins' mission would never be forgotten. It was intangible, and perhaps undefinable, yet very meaningful to his British hosts, especially to Churchill. On March 8, hours before the Lend Lease Bill passed and with Hopkins' words still fresh in his mind, Churchill lunched at Downing Street with Sir Arthur Salter who had just been appointed to head an important mission to the United States. Churchill quoted his guest a poem by Arthur Clough. The lines which most impressed Salter were:

> And not by Eastern windows only,
> When daylight comes, comes in the light.
> In front the sun climbs slow, how slowly
> But westward, look, the land is bright. [31]

Hopkins would see Churchill many times during the war. It was inevitable that misunderstandings and tensions would arise, but their friendship was never in doubt. His next visit was in less than 6 months. In July 1941, Hopkins saw Churchill both before and after his journey to Russia to meet with Stalin. Hopkins was present at all but one of the wartime meetings between Churchill and Roosevelt; however, none of his subsequent meetings with Churchill had the urgency or intimacy of their time together in early 1941. Hopkins had predicted that the United States' entry in the war would involve an incident with Japan; moreover, he knew the personal sacrifice that such a war might require. In February, 1944, United States Marines landed at Kwajalein. One of the Marines killed in this assault was Private First Class Stephen P. Hopkins. He was Hopkins' youngest son. Not long afterwards, Hopkins received a beautifully lettered scroll from Churchill. It was inscribed with words from the final scene of Macbeth:

> Stephen Peter Hopkins
> Age 18
>
> > *"Your son, my lord, has paid a soldier's debt:*
> > *He only liv'd but till he was a man;*
> >
> > *The which no sooner had his prowess confirm'd*
> > *In the unshrinking station where he fought,*
> > *But like a man he died"*
> >
> > Shakespeare
>
> To Harry Hopkins from Winston S. Churchill
> 13th February, 1944 [32]

In December 1944, Hopkins found himself in the midst of what might have become the most serious dispute between America and Great Britain of the entire war. A civil war had erupted in Greece following the German withdrawal. Churchill was determined to prevent the Communist guerrilla force known as ELAS from seizing power. On December 4, ELAS bands had taken over most of the police stations in Athens and murdered many policemen. The Greek government was desperate. At 4:50 in the morning on December 5, Churchill sent General Scobie, the local British commander, an unambiguous directive by telegram to suppress the Communists which included the following: "Do not however hesitate to act as if you were in a conquered city where a local rebellion is in progress." [33] When Admiral Ernest J. King, Commander in Chief of the U.S. Fleet, learned of the British action, he ordered the Navy to cease supplying British forces in Greece. This precipitous order may well have been influenced by King's "near-psychotic anglophobia." [34] The British reaction was prompt and predictable.

A furious Churchill called Hopkins in Washington on an open telephone line. Because the connection was bad, Hopkins could only make out two words, "Greece" and "Halifax," but the next morning in the map room of the White House he noticed a news summary stating that Admiral King had cut off supplies to the British in Greece. Hopkins immediately recognized that King had gotten into the political arena and that the order should be withdrawn as soon as possible. Admiral William D. Leahy, the president's chief of staff, who was then at the White House, concurred. At Hopkins' suggestion Leahy called Admiral King who without protest withdrew his order. This did not end the acrimony. Churchill was planning to send a strong protest to the president; however, Hopkins was able to convince Halifax that such a protest would only cause more trouble and was unnecessary because the matter had been settled in a way satisfactory to the British. In the end Churchill did not send the protest. An open breach in Anglo-American relations had been averted, in large measure due to Hopkins' good judgment and decisiveness.

The crisis in Greece and the German offensive in the Ardennes, among other problems, had made December a trying month for the British leader. Hopkins was not insensitive to the severe stress on the seventy-year-old Churchill. On December 21 he sent Churchill the following cable:

> Dear Winston: I want you to know on this fateful Christmas, that I am well aware of the heavy burdens you carry. Since our first meeting I have tried to share them with you. I would share them now.
>
> The raging battle and overhanging clouds are the prelude to a sure and glorious victory for us. What a gallant role you play in the greatest drama in the world's history. No one knows better than I.
>
> There are some of my countrymen who would destroy me by the assertion that I am your good friend. All I can say is that I am ever so proud that it is so.
>
> And you will know with what affection Louie and I send you and Clemmie our warmest Christmas greeting. [35]

The last time Churchill saw either Roosevelt or Hopkins was on February 15, 1945, on board the USS *Quincy* in Alexandria harbor four days after the adjournment of the Yalta Conference. Shortly before noon Churchill and his party came aboard to bid Roosevelt farewell. A small luncheon had been planned in

Churchill's honor. Besides Churchill and Roosevelt, the only others present were Anna Boettiger, the president's daughter; Sarah Oliver, the prime minister's daughter; Randolph Churchill, the prime minister's son; John G. Winant, the U.S. ambassador to Britain; Admiral William D. Leahy, the president's chief of staff, and Harry Hopkins. Of this occasion Churchill would later write:

> *We gathered afterwards in his cabin for an informal family luncheon. The President seemed placid and frail. I felt that he had a slender contact with life. I was not to see him again. We bade affectionate farewells.* [36]

It was fitting that Hopkins had been included in a family luncheon. For by then he was a cherished friend of the Churchill family. On his return to the United States Hopkins, who had lost eighteen pounds during the Yalta Conference, almost immediately proceeded to the Mayo Clinic. The seriousness of his condition required him to remain there for the better part of two months. He was still at Mayo's when Roosevelt suddenly died at Warm Springs, Georgia, on April 12. At this time of national grief few considered the magnitude of Hopkins' bereavement. Churchill was one of the few. He sent a message of condolence to Mrs. Roosevelt and another to Harry Hopkins, saying to the latter, "I understand how deep your feelings of grief must be." [37]

On Saturday morning, July 7, President Truman and the American delegation departed Newport News, Viriginia on the heavy cruiser *Augusta* for the summit meeting with Churchill and Stalin at Potsdam. Hopkins was not among the delegates. Five days earlier, for reasons of health, he had severed all ties with his government. Although Hopkins refrained from any public comment on the Potsdam conference, he was vitally interested and eager to get a firsthand account from his friend, Chip Bohlen, who was Truman's interpreter at his meetings with Stalin. During the conference the results of the British election were announced. Bohlen would later write, "We were all shocked by Churchill's defeat." [38] Churchill had flown back to England on July 26 to learn the next day that the British people had rejected his party and his leadership. In a letter to Beaverbrook dated July 28, Hopkins revealed his feelings about Churchill's political downfall: "He has been so gallant throughout this war that I find I am greatly dejected that this should happen to him at this time in his life." [39]

By the middle of October Hopkins' health was failing rapidly and he was confined at home. On January 22, 1946, Hopkins wrote from a hospital bed to Churchill, then on holiday in the United States with his wife and daughter, Sarah.

His words could only have pleased Churchill: "Do give my love to Clemmie and Sarah, all of whom I shall hope to see before you go back, but I want to have a good talk with you over the state of world affairs, to say nothing of our private lives." [40] It was too late for another meeting. Hopkins died on January 29, 1946, in New York's Memorial Hospital. He was 55 years old.

In early 1950 Churchill completed volume three of his history of the Second World War, entitled *The Grand Alliance*. Churchill was invariably gracious in his references to those Americans with whom he was in close contact during the war.

His tribute to Hopkins in *The Grand Alliance* is singularly gracious and moving:

> *At our first meeting we were about three hours together, and I soon comprehended his personal dynamism and the outstanding importance of his mission. This was the height of the London bombing, and many local worries imposed themselves upon us. But it was evident to me that here was an envoy from the President of supreme importance to our life. With gleaming eye and quiet, constrained passion he said:*
>
> *"The President is determined that we shall win the war together. Make no mistake about it.*
>
> *"He has sent me here to tell you that at all costs and by all means he will carry you through, no matter what happens to him there is nothing he will not do so far as he has human power."*
>
> *Everyone who came in contact with Harry Hopkins in the long struggle will confirm what I have set down about his remarkable personality. And from this hour began a friendship between us which sailed serenely over all earthquakes and convulsions. He was the most faithful and perfect channel of communications between the President and me. But far more than that, he was for several years the main prop and animator of Roosevelt himself. Together these two men, the one a subordinate without public office, the other commanding the mighty Republic, were capable of taking decisions of the highest consequences over the whole area of the English speaking world.*
>
> *Hopkins was, of course, jealous about his personal influence with his Chief and did not encourage American competitors. He therefore in some ways bore out the poet*

Gray's line, "A favourite has no friend."   But this was not my affair. There he sat, slim, frail, ill, but absolutely glowing with refined comprehension of the Cause. It was to be the defeat, ruin, and slaughter of Hitler, to the exclusion of all other purposes, loyalties, or aims. In the history of the United States, few brighter flames have burned.

Harry Hopkins always went to the root of the matter. I have been present at several great conferences, where twenty or more of the most important executive personages were gathered together. When the discussion flagged and all seemed baffled, it was on these occasions he would rap out the deadly question, "Surely, Mr. President, here is the point we have got to settle. Are we going to face it or not?" Faced it always was, and, being faced, was conquered. He was a true leader of men, and alike in ardour and in wisdom in times of crisis he has rarely been excelled. His love of the causes of the weak and poor was matched by his passion against tyranny, especially when tyranny was, for the time, triumphant. [41]

Part II

BRAVE JOURNEY

Loch Lomond is one of the most beloved lakes in all of Scotland. It inspired the well-known Scottish ballad of the same name which is said to have been composed by a follower of Bonnie Prince Charlie on the eve of the composer's execution. The loch itself is twenty-three miles in length and between half a mile and five miles wide. In the south, soft green hills slope down to its shore. In the north, high mountains, which the Scots call munros, overlook its "bon bonnie banks."

On the last Sunday in July 1941, Flight Lieutenant David C. McKinley, D.F.C. and the crew of *Catalina* W8416 of the RAF Coastal Command were taking their ease on Loch Lomond after weeks of patrolling the northwest approaches between Scotland and Iceland. McKinley was unaware that he was about to leave this idyllic loch for one of the most dramatic flights of World War II.

At four o'clock that Sunday afternoon a reconnaissance plane flew over Loch Lomond flashing a signal that the

Flight Lieutenant D. C. McKinley, who was hand picked to fly Hopkins to Russia, is shown here on November 6, 1944.

flight lieutenant was to return immediately to his base at Oban on the west coast of Scotland. There he was informed that he was to proceed the next day to Invergordon on Scotland's east coast for an urgent mission. At his briefing in Invergordon he learned that he was to fly three important persons from Invergordon to Archangel in Russia, which was at war with Nazi Germany after the most massive invasion in recorded history.

This mission was arranged by the British Prime Minister Winston Churchill, as a special favor to President Roosevelt. The most prominent passenger was an American named Harry

Lloyd Hopkins then almost fifty-one whose precarious health made such a long flight somewhat problematical. Prior to January of that year Churchill had never even heard of Hopkins. On January 10, 1941, Hopkins, as the personal envoy of Franklin Roosevelt, had called at No. 10 Downing Street on his first diplomatic assignment. During this five-week mission Churchill and Hopkins had forged a friendship which would prove to be of enormous benefit to both their countries.

In July 1941, Hopkins returned to England with several high-ranking American military officers to express a concern that the Middle East was absorbing such a large proportion of America's war supplies. Hopkins also wanted to apprise Churchill of Roosevelt's desire to meet him in the near future in some lonely bay guarded by British and American warships. Roosevelt had not planned for Hopkins to go to Russia. If it was not on his formal agenda, the Russian situation was much on Hopkins' mind. According to Churchill, "The first topic which he opened to me was the new situation created by Hitler's invasion of Russia." [42] A short time later Hopkins asked Churchill whether it was possible to fly to Moscow and return within one week. Churchill informed him that the RAF Coastal Command had recently commenced flights by PBY flying boats from Invergordon in Scotland around the north cape of Norway to Archangel, but Churchill was not enthusiastic about such a long and hazardous undertaking. Hopkins was undeterred. On Friday evening, July 25, he and the new American Ambassador, John G. Winant, drafted a cable to Roosevelt stating the rationale for the proposed mission which read in part:

> *I am wondering whether you would think it important and useful for me to go to Moscow. Air transportation good and can reach there in twenty four hours...If Stalin could in any way be influenced at a critical time I think it would be worth doing by a direct communication from you through a personal envoy. I think the stakes are so great that it should be done. Stalin would then know in an unmistakable way that we mean business on a long term supply job. I, of course, have made no moves in regard to this and await your advice. [43]*

Within twenty-four hours Roosevelt had approved Hopkins' mission, with a veiled reminder to return in time for the then top secret meeting between Roosevelt and Churchill. In the postwar years Hopkins' mentor has been severely criticized for putting too much trust in Stalin. Prior to Germany's invasion,

Roosevelt's opinion of Stalin was disclosed in a February 1940 speech denouncing Russia's aggression against Finland in these words:

> *The Soviet Union, as everybody who has the courage to face the fact knows, is run by a dictatorship as absolute as any of the dictatorships in the world. It has allied itself with another dictatorship and it has invaded a neighbor so infinitesimally small that it could do no conceivable possible harm to the Soviet Union, a neighbor which seeks only to live at peace as a democracy and a liberal, forward-looking democracy at that.* [44]

A year later Hopkins wrote to Mayor La Guardia, "I am enclosing photostats of a couple of communist documents which show the way they are operating on this. It just seems to me that we have got to find a way to beat these people. From my point of view they are just as much a potential enemy as the Germans." [45]

After the German invasion Roosevelt and Hopkins viewed the Soviet Union in a different light. The alacrity with which Roosevelt approved Hopkins' mission, notwithstanding inherent dangers, suggests that Roosevelt was anxious to get a firsthand report on the war situation, as well as Hopkins' personal assessment of the Russian dictator.

Of all the people with whom Hopkins conferred about this mission none was more important than Churchill. The British prime minister made all of the flight arrangements. More clearly than anyone he saw the urgency, the dangers, the drama, and the potential rewards of Hopkins' mission. In a short time these two had become very close. On Sunday evening, July 27, Hopkins was driven from Chequers to London's Euston Station where he caught a train for Invergordon. Before departing he and Churchill walked out on the lawn at Chequers. It was still light. Churchill bade his friend farewell with not a little emotion:

> *"Tell him, tell him," Churchill said. "Tell him that Britain has but one ambition today, but one desire—to crush Hitler. Tell him that he can depend upon us...Goodby—God bless you, Harry."* [46]

The responsibility for getting Hopkins to Russia fell squarely on the shoulders of twenty-eight-year-old Flight Lieutenant David McKinley. Although McKinley had experience with long range patrols over the North Atlantic, he had never flown around the North Cape of Norway to Archangel. The American-made

PBY, commonly known as the Catalina, was powered by two Pratt & Whitney radial, air-cooled engines which gave it a maximum speed of 175 mph at seven thousand feet. Fully loaded with fuel it could only manage 135 mph. Its main characteristics were dependability and long range, 2,350 miles.

To reach Archangel from Invergordon, McKinley would fly nonstop over two thousand miles. The chief risks were posed by German fighter aircraft based in Norway. The Luftwaffe had two fighter aircraft, the Messerschmitt Bf. 109 and the Messerschmitt Bf. 110, which had twice the speed of a PBY. The Bf. 110 was particularly dangerous because of its armament consisting of four machine guns and two 20mm cannon, all of which fired forward. Flight Lieutenant McKinley is now a retired air vice marshal living on Alderney in the Channel Islands. He has graciously corresponded with the author about Hopkins' journey. In response to a question about the problem of German fighter aircraft, he replied:

> I was attacked many times by German and Italian fighters in the Mediterranean and each time I dived to sea level where the fighters seemed unable to pull out and so plunged into the water. I would have tried like tactics had I been attacked on the Archangel route. [47]

Flight Lieutenant McKinley kept well away from the Norwegian Coast and never sighted any German planes or warships. After being airborne for twenty and a half hours the PBY landed at Archangel on the White Sea. To McKinley Hopkins appeared "very tired." [48] An attractive Soviet woman interpreter informed Hopkins that it would be impossible to fly him to Moscow that night and that his flight was scheduled to depart at 4:00 A.M. the next morning. That evening an admiral invited Hopkins and his party to dine aboard his yacht. Hopkins later described the evening as "monumental" with "course after course." It was his first experience with vodka, about which he observed:

> There was the inescapable cold fish, caviar, and vodka. Vodka has authority. It is nothing for the amateur to trifle with. [49]

With only two hours of sleep Hopkins was taken to the Archangel airport for the four-hour flight to Moscow. On arrival there the American ambassador, Laurence A. Steinhardt, took him to the official residence, Spaso House, and put him to bed, but Hopkins was too excited to sleep for long. Later in the day

Hopkins is greeted at the Moscow Airport by Ambassador Laurence A. Steinhardt on July 30, 1941.

Courtesy of the Franklin D. Roosevelt Library

Hopkins had a long talk with the American ambassador. In the early evening Hopkins, Steinhardt, and an interpreter named Reinhardt, left Spaso House for the Kremlin.

During the war Americans called Stalin "Uncle Joe." To many he seemed a benign, avuncular figure who led a heroic struggle against Nazi Germany. The fact that Stalin was a ruthless tyrant directly responsible for the deaths of millions was not generally known. Hopkins undoubtedly knew more than most.

Hopkins' meeting with Stalin commenced without fanfare. After an exchange of greetings, Hopkins told Stalin that President Roosevelt believed that the most important thing to be done in the world was to defeat Hitler and Hitlerism. He went on to say that the president and the American government were determined to extend all possible aid to the Soviet Union as soon as possible.

After Stalin welcomed Hopkins to the Soviet Union, he made it clear that he had already been informed of the reason for his visit. Stalin then told Hopkins that the present leaders of Germany knew no minimum moral standard and that they represented an antisocial force in the world. Hopkins hardly needed to be told this, even if it was the standard communist line.

In his usual way Hopkins got straight to the point asking Stalin what his immediate military needs and long range requirements were. Without hesitation Stalin said the Soviet military needed (1) twenty thousand antiaircraft guns, (2) heavy machine guns for the defense of cities, and (3) one million or more rifles. The long range needs were high octane aviation gasoline and aluminum for aircraft production.

Hopkins made no comment about America's ability to fill this order, but he did remind Stalin that two hundred Curtis P-40s were on the way and one of the officers who had come with him to Moscow was an expert on that type of aircraft. They then discussed various routes for shipping supplies to the Soviet Union. Stalin favored Archangel over Vladivostok or the Persian Gulf.

Toward the end of their meeting Hopkins informed Stalin that his stay in Moscow had to be brief and he politely asked if the Russian leader would prefer discussions with Hopkins to be handled by other representatives of the Soviet government. Stalin replied, "You are our guest; you have but to command," adding that he would be available to meet with Hopkins from 6:00 to 7:00 P.M. each night. [50] Their first meeting, which had lasted two hours, was cordial, somewhat formal, and not particularly informative about the situation on the Russian front.

The following evening, July 31, Hopkins went to the Kremlin alone. The only other person present was Maxim Litvinov, the erstwhile commissar for foreign affairs, who late in 1941 would become ambassador to the United States. It is probable that the absence of any other American made Stalin less inhibited. In any event, it proved to be a much more interesting encounter.

Courtesy of the Franklin D. Roosevelt Library

Hopkins and Stalin at the Kremlin on July 31, 1941.

At the outset Hopkins told Stalin that the president was anxious to have his appreciation of the war between Germany and Russia. Stalin was well prepared. He gave Hopkins details of the respective German and Russian divisional strengths, saying that he believed that Germany could mobilize three hundred divisions, whereas Russia could mobilize three hundred fifty divisions by the following spring. Stalin asserted that the present front was a "far more propitious one" than a defensive line near Russia's western border. [51]

Stalin pointedly told Hopkins that Russian forces were not concerned that German armor had penetrated the front lines because of the Russian capacity to fight behind the Germans and to break out at night, adding that "this accounts for the fact that there have been no mass surrenders of troops on either side." [52] He repeatedly mentioned to Hopkins the difficulty the Germans would have protecting overextended supply lines and in transporting fuel to their panzer divisions' forward positions. Regarding tanks Stalin emphasized that his largest tanks were better than the German tanks except for their seventy-ton tanks which he discounted because of the poor roads and the Russian bridges which could not hold their weight.

Stalin launched a lengthy monologue concerning the relative strengths of the two opposing air forces. He acknowledged that the Germans had a powerful air force, but he thought that they underrated the Red Air Force. He told Hopkins that they had seven or eight thousand older-type fighters which had been very useful and successful against many of the German planes. He went on to say that they had approximately two thousand newer-type fighters at the front consisting of three different models. He also mentioned three new models of medium bombers without specifying any numbers, and three types of long range bombers of which he asserted they had six hundred.

He dismissed German claims of Soviet air losses as absurd, but would not indicate the actual number of Soviet planes that had been destroyed. In his report to the president, Hopkins related all of Stalin's statements concerning the size and strength of the Red Air Force concluding with the comment, "No information given above was confirmed by any other source." [53]

His second and final meeting with Stalin had lasted three hours. Stalin had demonstrated a masterful knowledge of Russia's needs. He had been confident about the war situation, but had been careful not to appear overconfident. He clearly wanted to make a favorable impression on Hopkins and there is no doubt he had. Later Hopkins described Stalin in the *American* magazine:

> *There was no waste of word, gesture, nor mannerism. It was like talking to a perfectly co-ordinated machine, an intelligent machine. Joseph Stalin knew what he wanted, knew what Russia wanted and assumed that you knew...No man could forget the picture of the dictator of Russia as he stood watching me leave—an austere, rugged, determined figure in boots that shone like mirrors, stout, baggy trousers, and snug-fitting blouse. He wore no ornament, military or civilian. He's built close to the ground like a football coach's dream of a tackle. He's about five feet six, about a hundred and ninety pounds. His hands are huge, as hard as his mind.* [54]

Hopkins had no way of knowing that Stalin's virtuosic performance was based on a concoction of half truths, egregious misrepresentations, and glaring omissions. Stalin had told Hopkins there had been no mass surrender of troops on either side. This was simply not true, as Stalin well knew. Just before the invasion most of the forces in the Western Military District under the command of General Dmitry Pavlov were situated far to the west in a salient that jutted into German-held Poland. By June 26, five days into the invasion, Guderian's 2nd Panzer Group was 175 miles inside Russia. Two days later the 2nd Panzer Group and the 3rd Panzer Group, under Colonel General Herman Hoth, completed a double envelopment of Minsk. The Russian 3rd and 10th Armies as well as elements of three other armies were trapped in the Bialystok salient.

Although the Russian army made desperate attempts to break out, their efforts were largely futile due to a lack of air cover and the overall disorganization of the Soviet forces. Pavlov had already made a serious mistake by committing his reserves to a counterattack against German infantry, not realizing that he was about to be enveloped by two panzer groups. He was only able to avoid being captured himself by shifting his headquarters from Minsk to Mogilev, some one hundred miles to the east. There he was called by the Russian chief of staff, Zhukov, who wanted to know whether there was "some measure of truth" [55] to the German claims that they had surrounded two armies east of Bialystok.

"Yes," Pavlov answered, "a large measure of truth." [56] He and several of his aides were immediately ordered to Moscow and shot. This disaster had cost the Russian army 280,000 prisoners.

Stalin had also told Hopkins that German claims of Russian losses in combat aircraft were "absurd." [57] Stalin knew better. At sunrise on June 22, the Luftwaffe hit 66 airfields containing nearly three-fourths of the Soviet combat aircraft. By the end of that day the Luftwaffe had destroyed 1,811 Soviet planes, 1,489 on the ground and 322 in the air. During the next twenty-four hours another 1,000 aircraft were destroyed, most of which were bombers. The Russian high command had foolishly ordered Soviet bomber forces to attack German targets in Poland and elsewhere without fighter escorts. The result was a disaster which cost the Red Air Force over 500 bombers. Their commander, Lieutenant General Kopets, subsequently killed himself. By the end of the first week of the war Soviet losses had mounted to 4,017 aircraft. Aviation historian Von Hardesty has written, "For the Soviets it was an air debacle of unprecedented scope and devastation." [58]

Among his other misrepresentations, Stalin had told Hopkins that the Soviets possessed seven or eight thousand older-type fighters, two thousand of the newer-type fighters, an unspecified number of medium bomber types, and six hundred long range bombers. The best estimates are that the Russian Air Force had between seven and ten thousand combat aircraft before the war, which made it the world's largest. At the end of the first week the Russians had lost 4,017 aircraft; between then and September they were losing aircraft in combat at the average of fifty-five aircraft a day; hundreds of others must have been lost in accidents. By the end of July the Soviets probably had fewer than three thousand combat aircraft that were operational, rather than the ten thousand or more that Stalin claimed.

Stalin shrewdly realized that if he made an honest disclosure concerning the very serious, though far from hopeless, plight of the Russian forces, Roosevelt might well write off Russia as a lost cause and direct all subsequent aid to Britain. As impressive as he was during his second meeting with Hopkins, Stalin could not entirely conceal his deepest concerns.

At one point in their second meeting Stalin told Hopkins that it would be much better if Russia's tanks could be manufactured in the United States. Considering the distances, the lack of shipping, and the difficulties of mass producing an entirely new line of tanks, it was an astonishing suggestion. Toward the end of their second meeting Stalin made a final appeal which can only be called desperate. He indicated that the United States should join the war against Hitler, telling Hopkins that "it would be very difficult for Britain and Russia combined to crush the German military machine." [59] Hopkins quickly responded that his "mission related entirely to matters of supply and that the matter of our joining in the war would be decided largely by Hitler himself and his encroachment on our fundamental interests." [60]

When Hopkins prepared his report to President Roosevelt, he divided it into three parts. Only Part III made any reference to Stalin's desire to have the United States enter the war. It was marked "For the President Only." [61] Hopkins suggested in his cover letter that no copy be sent to the State Department.

Harry Hopkins' mission to Moscow ended on August 1, 1941. He had assured Stalin that the United States and Britain would "do everything possible in the succeeding weeks to send material to Russia." [62] He had hedged any commitments by telling Stalin that obviously the material had to have been already manufactured. He further conditioned the delivery of heavy equipment including tanks, aircraft, and antiaircraft guns on a conference to be held by representatives of the American, British, and Russian governments as soon as the front had stabilized. On August 1, the Soviet newspaper *Izvestiya* gave the Stalin-Hopkins meetings front page coverage with a large photograph of the two men standing side-by-side.

While his two meetings with Stalin took precedence over all else, Hopkins made the most of his stay in Moscow. On July 31,

The front page of Izvestiya on August 1, 1941

Hopkins met with the British ambassador, Sir Stafford Cripps. That afternoon Hopkins called on the Commissar of Foreign Affairs, V. M. Molotov, who had made the announcement to the Russian people over Radio Moscow of the German invasion over nine hours after the event, when Stalin was temporarily unable to function. After his earlier meeting with Stalin, Hopkins had been permitted to speak with one Russian general, a General Yakovlev, an artilleryman of the Red Army. The general was aware that anything he said might be repeated to Stalin. When Hopkins quizzed him about the specific needs of the Russian forces then heavily engaged with the panzers, his response revealed something of the current frame of mind among Russian generals. After first telling Hopkins that "the Russians could use extra tanks and antitank guns," he appeared to have second thoughts and quickly added, "I am not empowered to say whether we do or do not need tanks or anti-tank guns." [63]

Hopkins rejoined Flight Lieutenant McKinley and the crew of his PBY at Archangel in the late afternoon of August 1, after a flight from Moscow during which the Russian pilot exhibited his skills by buzzing the airstrip prior to landing. The extent that this mission had depleted Hopkins' physical strength is manifest from a brief conversation with McKinley. The British pilot thought Hopkins "looked very tired and ill" and asked him whether "he wished to remain a little longer and rest before attempting the journey." [64] Hopkins declined this suggestion, commenting that "whatever the next twenty-four hours may bring it cannot be as trying as the last three days." [65] Late on the afternoon of August 1, McKinley took off into a gathering storm and headed up the White Sea. Besides the flight crew of five, the PBY carried three passengers and a large quantity of platinum.

McKinley would unavoidably fly within a hundred miles of the German air bases at Petsamo in Finland and at Kirkenes in Norway. Forty-eight hours earlier two British carriers had carried out airstrikes against targets in these areas during which the Germans had managed to destroy almost one-third of the attacking aircraft with minimal losses to themselves. Earlier Churchill had cabled Stalin, "We have asked your staff to keep a certain area clear of Russian vessels between July 28 and August 2, when we shall hope to strike." [66] By August 1, the aircraft carriers had withdrawn from the Kirkenes-Petsamo area, but the Luftwaffe was almost certainly still on maximum alert.

In his report Flight Lieutenant McKinley wrote, "Whilst proceeding up the Murman Coast and still east of Kola Inlet we were fired upon by unidentified warships of a typical destroyer class." [67] McKinley immediately passed the necessary recognition signal then used by the Russian Navy; however, the firing did not cease until he had flown beyond the range of the ships' guns. Although the Germans had a flotilla of destroyers based at Kirkenes, McKinley believes these warships were Russian. This was their only hostile encounter during their twenty-four hour flight to Scapa Flow. Most of the time Hopkins slept. He was suffering from extreme exhaustion and from lack of the medicine and food supplements which he was supposed to take every day without fail. Unfortunately, he had left these items in Moscow. After landing with considerable difficulty on the choppy waters of Scapa Flow, McKinley found it impossible to taxi his aircraft close enough to the naval launch which had been dispatched for Hopkins. McKinley recounted his last view of Hopkins:

> *At this stage Mr. Hopkins had to make a hazardous leap from the aircraft to the launch followed by his luggage which was literally hurled across the several yards of open water separating us from the launch. My last glimpse of him showed him smiling and determined, though very dishevelled as the result of his wearying experience. As he waved us farewell we could not help feeling that very few persons could have taken what he had endured since we met at Invergordon on July 28. Circling overhead prior to our return flight to Oban we saw a launch wallowing heavily across the harbour and we wondered if there was to be any rest for a man so obviously ill and yet showing unbelievable courage, determination and appreciation for the services of others.* [68]

The date was Saturday, August 2, 1941. In two days Churchill was scheduled to arrive at Scapa Flow to board HMS *Prince of Wales* for his voyage across the Atlantic to meet Roosevelt at Placentia Bay on the coast of Newfoundland. That night at dinner on the *Prince of Wales*, Hopkins was in a state of near collapse. Admiral Sir John Tovey summoned all of the medical skill available. Hopkins was put to bed, medicated, and permitted to sleep until the following afternoon. Hopkins was starting to revive when Churchill arrived late the next afternoon. Churchill has described their reunion:

> *Before darkness fell on August 4 the* Prince of Wales *with her escort of destroyers steamed out into the broad waters of the Atlantic. I found Harry Hopkins much exhausted by his long air journeys and exacting confer-*

ences in Moscow. Indeed, he had arrived at Scapa two days before in such a condition that the Admiral had put him to bed at once and kept him there. Nevertheless, he was as gay as ever, gathered strength slowly during the voyage and told me all about his mission. [69]

Although he apparently never questioned Stalin's duplicity concerning Russia's losses in aircraft and in men, Hopkins was able to appreciate certain vital factors regarding that then remote communist nation. He sensed the courage of the individual Russian soldier and the determination of the Russian people to defend their homeland. More significantly, Hopkins recognized that Stalin possessed the ruthlessness to wage war at whatever costs in human life and material resources. All of this he imparted to Churchill. The core of Hopkins' message was simple and direct. The Russians were putting up a terrific fight and America and Britain should help them all they could. His basic assumption was that the Red Army would withstand the German onslaught. Any assessment of the significance of Hopkins' mission needs to take account of the conventional military wisdom that prevailed in both Washington and London.

According to the British historian Paul Johnson, in mid-1939 the British and French chiefs of staff "rated the Soviet army below Poland; and if it came to a choice (they) would opt for the latter." [70] The Winter War between Russia and Finland seemed to confirm their most serious doubts. American military authorities were no more sanguine about the Russian army than the British and French. Shortly after the Germans invaded Russia, secretary of war, Henry L. Stimson, wrote the president that General Marshall and the men in the War Plans Division were in substantial agreement that it would take Germany a "possible maximum of three months" to beat Russia. [71] Churchill would later write, "Almost all responsible military opinion held that the Russian armies would soon be defeated and largely destroyed." [72]

Hopkins was the first Western leader to reach Moscow after the German invasion. His report undoubtedly reassured Churchill and Roosevelt that their decision to aid Russia was well founded. Perhaps, more importantly, he was able to dispel the doubts that the American and British military chiefs still harbored about the Russian army. In his book, *Roosevelt and Hopkins*, Robert E. Sherwood called Hopkins' journey, "one of the most extraordinarily important and valuable missions of the whole war." [73] In the hindsight of over fifty years Sherwood's assessment holds true. For its time it was also an extraordinarily long and arduous journey fraught with peril for Harry L. Hopkins, for Flight Lieutenant David C. McKinley, for his crew, and for the other passengers. It was, indeed, a brave journey.

Part III

CONFRONTATION IN LONDON

On July 16, 1942, Franklin Roosevelt, as Commander in Chief, issued a written order to Harry L. Hopkins, his closest foreign policy adviser, to General George C. Marshall, Chief of Staff of the United States Army and to Admiral Ernest J. King, Commander in Chief United States Navy and Chief of Naval Operations. Their order stated, "You will proceed immediately to London as my personal representatives for the purpose of consultation with appropriate British authorities on the conduct of the war." [74] George Catlett Marshall was more than the highest ranking officer in the United States Army and the senior member of the Joint Chiefs of Staff. On both sides of his family he descended from settlers who had been in Virginia from the 17th century. He had graduated from the Virginia Military Institute where he held the highest cadet rank for each of his last three years. He possessed extraordinary presence. Dean Acheson, who was never overawed by the top brass, wrote of Marshall:

> *The moment General Marshall entered a room everyone in it felt his presence. It was a striking and communicated force. His figure conveyed intensity, which his voice, low, staccato, and incisive, reinforced. It compelled respect. It spread a sense of authority and of calm. There was no military glamour about him and nothing of the martinet.* [75]

Hopkins, Marshall, and King, who first learned of their mission the day before, flew out of Washington at noon on July 16 for Prestwick, Scotland, with an intermediate stop at Gander Lake, Newfoundland. During their extended journey each of them had ample time to reflect on their mission and to ponder the series of defeats that had so recently beset the Allies.

In May and early June the Afrika Korps led by General Edwin Rommel had driven British forces out of Cyrenaica toward the Egyptian frontier. The British had held a redoubt around the port of Tobruk which the panzers bypassed. This fortress was defended by four infantry brigades, a tank brigade, a reconnaissance battalion, plus six regiments of artillery. This formidable force under the command of General Klopper, a South African, was provisioned with enough supplies and ammunition for sixty days. Auchinleck, the British Middle East commander, planned to hold Tobruk as a thorn in the side of the Afrika Korps until a British counteroffensive could be launched.

The year before, Tobruk had been a symbol of courage and defiance. It had held out for 242 days after being cut off from the main British army. The siege of Tobruk ended on December 9, 1941 when the German-Italian forces were pushed westward. In 1942 the British deployment at Tobruk was larger and better equipped than it had been in 1941. Churchill and the British chiefs of staff fully expected Tobruk to hold.

Their expectations were shattered by Rommel. On June 17 his armored columns decimated the 4th Armored Brigade at an obscure desert site called Sidi Rezegh, forty miles southeast of Tobruk. Afterwards the British had insufficient tanks to mount any serious relief of the Tobruk garrison. Sometime around 6:30 A.M. on June 20, the 21st Panzer Division, supported by the 15th Panzer Division and the Italian Armored Division, together with a motorized infantry division, struck that part of the Tobruk defense held by the 11th Indian Brigade. By noon German tanks had broken the British lines and were heading north and west outflanking the 4th South African Brigade. At 2:00 A.M. on June 21, General Klopper spoke by radio-telephone to General Ritchie, the commander of the British Eighth Army, apprising him that the situation was a "shambles." The South African General was faced with the terrible choice of either allowing the panzers to slaughter his virtually helpless garrison or capitulating. Reluctantly he chose capitulation, which took place at 7:45 A.M. on June 21. Thirty-three thousand British and Commonwealth troops were taken prisoner.

Within a week Rommel had exploited his victory by launching a renewed offensive aimed directly at the Nile Delta and the Suez Canal. By June 30, Rommel's forces had reached Alamein only sixty miles from the port of Alexandria. This forced the British Fleet to evacuate their base and withdraw into the Red Sea, out of range of German divebombers.

Four days after the fall of Tobruk, a conservative M.P., Sir John Wardlaw-Milne, placed a vote of censure before the British Parliament in the following terms:

> *That this house, while paying tribute to the heroism and endurance of the Armed Forces of the Crown in circumstances of exceptional difficulty, has no confidence in the central direction of the war.* [76]

During the debate Harold Nicolson wrote in his diary, "Winston sits there with a look of sullen foreboding, his face from time to time flickering into a smile." [77] Churchill had retained the right to speak last. When he arose to address the house on July 2, his words were grave:

> The military misfortunes of the last fortnight in Cyrenaica and Egypt have completely transformed the situation, not only in this theatre but throughout the Mediterranean. We have lost upwards of fifty thousand men, by far the larger proportion of whom are prisoners, a great mass of material, and in spite of carefully organized demolitions, large quantities of stores have fallen into the enemy's hands. Rommel has advanced nearly four hundred miles through the desert and is now approaching the fertile Delta of the Nile. The evil effects of these events in Turkey, Spain, in France, and in French North Africa, cannot yet be measured. We are at this moment in the presence of a recession of our hopes and prospects in the Middle East and in the Mediterranean unequaled since the fall of France. [78]

Due to his honesty and his eloquence, and to some extent to the ineptness of his opponents, Churchill easily survived this vote of censure by a margin of four hundred seventy-five to twenty-five. That same night his friend, Harry Hopkins, cabled from Washington:

> Action at Commons today delighted me. These have been some of the bad days. No doubt there will be others. They who run for cover with every reverse, the timid and faint of heart, will have no part in winning the war. Your strength, tenacity, and everlasting courage will see Britain through, and the President, you know, does not quit. I know you are of good heart, for your military defeats and ours and our certain victories to come will be shared together. More power to you. [79]

"The bad days" which Hopkins mentioned included far more than the Middle East Crisis. On June 23 the Germans had broken the Russian lines on a wide front and begun their drive to the Volga and Caucasus. The critical situation on the southern Russian front was compounded by the difficulty of shipping badly needed supplies to Russia through their northernmost port of Murmansk. On July 4 and 5, Convoy P.Q. 17 bound for Murmansk was attacked in the Barents Sea by U-boats and aircraft. Of the thirty-five ships which left Iceland on June 27, twenty-three were sunk with few survivors plucked from the icy seas. Fourteen of the ships sunk were American. Churchill later called it, "one of the most melancholy naval episodes in the whole of the war." [80]

While the difficulties and dangers inherent in running convoys around the North Cape of Norway into Murmansk were well known, another potential threat was virtually unknown to the American and British publics. By June 1942, the Finns, who were co-belligerents with Germany rather than formal allies, had retaken several thousand square miles of their own country and had advanced into the Russian province of Eastern Karelia. Finland, under Field Marshall Mannerheim, possessed one of the finest small armies in the world. In June 1942 the Finns were in a position to sever the only rail link between Murmansk and the interior of Russia by seizing the town of Belomorsk on the White Sea. Earlier, Mannerheim's army had cut the railroad connecting Murmansk and Leningrad. On May 25 Mannerheim had confided to his friend, Ambassador G. A. Gripenberg, that Finnish forces should naturally take Belomorsk, but that it was now impossible because of the United States. The Finns had been explicitly warned by Secretary of State Hull that any interference with American shipments of supplies to Russia would have the gravest consequences. Despite German pressure, the Finns refused to cut this vital rail link and the United States never declared war on Finland.

Besides the disaster in the Middle East and the crisis in Russia, there was for Britain the most crucial battle of all, the battle of the Atlantic. After the war Churchill wrote of that battle, "The Battle of the Atlantic was the dominating factor all through the war. Never for one moment could we forget that everything happening elsewhere, on land, at sea, or in the air, depended ultimately on its outcome and amid all other cares we viewed its changing fortunes day by day with hope or apprehension." [81] In June 1942, the Allies were losing the Battle of the Atlantic. In that month shipping losses from U-boats and other enemy action exceeded 823,000 gross tons which involved the sinking of 170 Allied ships. In no other month of the war would losses be so heavy.

Against this backdrop of disasters and the potential for even greater disasters, on July 10, President Roosevelt received a stunning memorandum from his highest-ranking military chiefs. General Marshall and Admiral King, who had been dismayed to learn a few days earlier that the British War Cabinet were adamantly opposed to a cross-channel invasion of France in

1942, code-named SLEDGEHAMMER, seemed ready to discard the basic Anglo-American strategy of defeating Germany first. Their memorandum read in part:

> *If the United States is to engage in any other operation than forceful, unswerving, adherence to full Bolero plan (which included a possible 1942 cross-channel invasion) we are definitely of the opinion that we should turn to the Pacific and strike decisively against Japan. In other words, assume a defensive attitude against Germany, except for air operations and use all available means in the Pacific.* [82]

Long after the war Marshall told his biographer, Forrest C. Pogue, that, "In my case it was a bluff, but King wanted the (Pacific) alternative." [83] Robert Sherwood, who was working in the White House at the time, would later write, "The Hopkins papers shed no light on it, but it is my impression that the plan was far more than a bluff in General Marshall's mind and certainly in Admiral King's." [84] There was, in fact, little chance of the United States adopting a Pacific strategy. Roosevelt, as Commander in Chief, was steadfast in his conviction that the Allies should first defeat their strongest enemy, Germany. Roosevelt was willing to overrule Marshall and King on their recommendation to concentrate on the Pacific War first. He was not as willing to oppose them on their insistence on launching a cross-channel invasion of France in 1942 even though his preference was an operation against French North Africa. His memorandum to Hopkins, Marshall, and King, which they considered an order from their commander in chief, read in part:

> *5. In regard to 1942, you will carefully investigate the possibility of executing SLEDGEHAMMER. Such an operation would definitely sustain Russia this year. It might be the turning point which would save Russia this year. SLEDGEHAMMER is of such grave importance that every reason calls for accomplishment of it. You should strongly urge immediate all-out preparation for it, that it be pushed with the utmost vigor, and that it be executed whether or not Russian collapse becomes imminent. In the event Russian collapse becomes probable SLEDGEHAMMER becomes not merely advisable but imperative. The principal objective of SLEDGEHAMMER is the positive diversion of German Air Forces from the Russian Front.*

6. Only if you are completely convinced that SLEDGE-HAMMER is impossible of execution with reasonable chances of serving its intended purpose, inform me. [85]

While these two paragraphs indicate that Roosevelt was in agreement with Marshall and King, he also emphasized the vital importance of holding the Middle East. Paragraph 8 of this document reads:

8. The Middle East should be held as strongly as possible whether Russia collapses or not.

• • •

8. (8) You will determine the best methods of holding the Middle East. These methods include definitely either or both of the following:
a. Sending aid and ground forces to the Persian Gulf, to Syria, and to Egypt.
b. A new operation in Morocco and Algiers [sic] intended to drive in against the backdoor of Rommel's armies. The attitude of French Colonial troops is still in doubt. [86]

What was obvious to the president and all of his advisors was that the Allies could not conduct both a cross-channel invasion of France and a North African operation in 1942. What was not so obvious to Marshall and King were the political implications of a failure of a cross-channel invasion. Roosevelt and Hopkins were more sensitive to the political risks to Churchill of another disaster; however, if Roosevelt had flatly refused to consider SLEDGEHAMMER, he would have had to face potential political risk of his own. It is not inconceivable that General Marshall would have resigned which would have certainly brought a torrent of criticism on the president. He resolved his dilemma by deciding to send Hopkins, Marshall, and King to London to confer with Churchill and the British chiefs of staff. If they could convince the British to agree to a cross-channel invasion in 1942, well and good. If they could not, then they would have to reach agreement on an alternative strategy. The president's foremost concerns were expressed in the last two paragraphs of his memorandum which read:

10. Please remember three cardinal principles—speed of decision on plans, unity of plans, attack combined with defense but not defense alone. This affects the immediate objective of U.S. ground forces fighting against Germans in 1942.

11. *I hope for total agreement within one week of your arrival.* [87]

Roosevelt had been aware for weeks that there was little hope of gaining British approval for a cross-channel invasion in 1942. Churchill had seemed to favor it when Hopkins and Marshall were in London the previous April; however, the more the British

Courtesy of the George C. Marshall Foundation

Hopkins with General George C. Marshall and Ambassador John G. Winant at the White House on April 20, 1942

chiefs of staff looked at the operation, the less they liked it. Churchill became convinced it would be a disaster with mostly British casualties because the United States could only contribute two divisions before October. During his June visit to the United States, Churchill had apprised Roosevelt of British concerns about SLEDGEHAMMER in a memorandum hand-delivered to the president at Hyde Park. After returning to England, Churchill sent Roosevelt a cable, the first sentence of which stated the British position in the plainest terms:

Former Naval Person to President Roosevelt—8 July 42

No responsible British general, admiral, or air marshal is prepared to recommend "SLEDGEHAMMER" as a practicable operation in 1942. [88]

This cable, while frank and to the point, did not fully reveal the depth of Churchill's opposition to a cross-channel invasion in 1942. Perhaps no one has described this any better than his personal physician, Sir Charles Wilson, who had joined him on his journey to America and who saw him frequently thereafter: "When the Americans came into the war after Pearl Harbour they began to plan for the day when the Allied armies would land again upon the French shore. It was General Marshall's conviction that only in that way could the war be won. Mr. Churchill was as sure that only by the premature invasion of France could the war be lost. To postpone that evil day, all his arts, all his eloquence, all his great experience were spent." [89]

General Marshall was willing to accept all the incalculable risks of a cross-channel invasion in 1942, in part, because of his concerns over a Russian collapse. During his life Marshall eschewed any self-justification of his actions as chief of staff. He rejected writing his autobiography. After much reluctance he finally agreed to allow Forrest C. Pogue to write an authorized biography. Pogue's first interview with Marshall took place September 28, 1956 at the Pentagon, where Marshall, as a retired five-star general, had been given an office which he seldom used. Pogue had only met the general a few days before at General and Mrs. Marshall's home in Leesburg and the two were still getting to know one another. Marshall was then in his 76th year but his memory was excellent. After lunch at the secretary of defense's dining room, they got down to work.

Early in the first interview, the subject of SLEDGEHAMMER came up. The following excerpts from Pogue's notes reveal much of Marshall's concerns about the Russian situation: "SLEDGEHAMMER was a desperate operation to save Russia...Russian army was in dire straits though and we had hoped to take off the pressure...The Russian army seemed headed for destruction...One sentence in our argument was that it would be a historic blunder if we allowed the Russian army to perish in the field...Looked like the Russians were going to be destroyed." [90]

Marshall's Air Staff had apparently advised him that a cross-channel invasion would lure a substantial part of the Luftwaffe into France where the Allies would have an opportunity to destroy it. At a White House meeting on May 30, Marshall told V. M. Molotov, the Russian Commissar of Foreign Affairs, who had come to the United States on Stalin's orders to argue for a second front in 1942, that the American strategy would be to invade France with a large enough ground force to provoke an all-out battle for "the destruction of the German air-force." [91]

Later, Marshall would become more skeptical of his inexperienced Air advisers. His only comment to Pogue about their role in SLEDGEHAMMER was, "The Air was virtually all talk and quite too much talk." [92]

Faced with the unanimous opposition of the British military leaders and Churchill, Marshall needed all the support he could muster. Admiral King would prove to be of limited help because of his acerbic manner and his tendency toward anglophobia. After the war King wrote his book, *Fleet Admiral King A Naval Record*, in which he stated, "King welcomed the opportunity of a showdown with the British regarding operations in 1942, for he felt that time was slipping away while tentative decisions were being first made and then reversed." [93]

Admiral Sir Andrew Browne Cunningham of the Royal Navy had arrived in Washington on June 24 as the representative of the First Sea Lord on the Combined Chiefs of Staff Committee. Cunningham, one of the most decorated of all British admirals, was soon in contact with King and Marshall. He would later write:

> I saw a good deal of Admiral Ernest King, my American opposite number. A man of immense capacity and ability, quite ruthless in his methods. He was not an easy person to get on with. He was tough and liked to be considered tough and at times became rude and overbearing...General Marshall I liked and admired immensely. One did not need to be long in his company before recognizing his sincerity and honesty of purpose. He could be obstinate enough; but would always listen to another point of view. [94]

If anyone could convince Churchill to support SLEDGEHAMMER, it was Harry Hopkins, who probably had more rapport with Churchill than any other American. Furthermore, Hopkins had the confidence and respect of General Marshall. While Hopkins' enemies in the United States were legion, Marshall was never among them. On Christmas Eve 1941, he wrote Hopkins, "You have been a source of confidence and assurance to me ever since our first meeting and conversation in December 1938." [95] Two weeks before their hurried departure for London, the general learned that Hopkins was engaged to be married to Mrs. Louise Macy of New York. He took time to write her about Hopkins.

> To be very frank, I am intensely interested in Harry's health and happiness, and therefore, in your approaching marriage. He has been gallant and self-sacrificing to an

> *extreme, little of which is realized by any but his most inti-*
> *mate friends. He is of great importance to our National*
> *interests at the present time, and is one of the most impru-*
> *dent people regarding his health that I have ever known.*
> *Therefore, and possibly inexcusable as it may seem to you,*
> *I express the hope that you will find it possible to curb his*
> *indiscretions and see that he takes the necessary rest.* [96]

The mission arrived by air at Prestwick in the early hours of Saturday, July 18. Churchill had provided a special train for his distinguished guests and had sent his aide, Commander Thompson, to welcome them. Thompson promptly informed them that Churchill wanted them to spend the balance of the weekend at Chequers, the prime minister's country residence. Injudiciously General Marshall and Admiral King, who were anxious to meet the American military in London, turned down Churchill's invitation. When their train arrived at London's Euston station at 7:50 A.M. they were greeted in person by General Sir Alan F. Brooke, Chief of the Imperial General Staff. By 10:00 A.M. they were installed at Claridge's Hotel and hard at work with General Eisenhower, head of the American Staff in Britain, and with Admiral Stark, King's predecessor as Chief of Naval Operations and the commander of United States Naval Forces Europe.

Hopkins was the first to learn that Churchill was upset with their refusal to spend the weekend with him. One telephone conversation convinced him that he needed to make amends by going immediately to Chequers where he spent most of Sunday assuring Churchill that no offense was intended. Afterwards, he reported to Roosevelt, "The Prime Minister threw the British Constitution at me with some vehemence. As you know, it is an unwritten document so no serious damage was done. Winston is his old self and full of battle." [97]

General Brooke had dined with Churchill at Chequers on Saturday evening. The other chiefs, Admiral of the Fleet Sir Dudley Pound, the First Sea Lord; Air Chief Marshal, Sir Charles F. A. Portal, Chief of the Air Staff, and Vice Admiral the Lord Louis Mountbatten, Chief of Combined Operations, were among the guests. The three Americans were conspicuous by their absence. Brooke recorded in his diary entry of the next day that Churchill "had informed me at Chequers that Marshall was trying to assume powers of Commander-in-Chief of American troops which was the President's prerogative." [98] This remark was never explained by Churchill, but it does indicate that

Churchill knew of some basic disagreement between the president and his chief of staff.

Marshall and King held their initial meeting with the British chiefs at 3:00 P.M. on Monday, July 20th after lunch at 10 Downing Street and a preliminary meeting with Churchill at which the prime minister told the Americans, "The first question was SLEDGEHAMMER. Should we do it or not? And if so, in what form? We, ourselves, had failed to devise a satisfactory plan but we would give the most earnest and sympathetic attention to any American Plan." [99]

In their first meeting with the British chiefs Marshall and King advocated the following plan: "...and that it (SLEDGEHAMMER) be regarded as the opening phase of ROUNDUP with the purpose of remaining on the Continent. This concept of establishing a bridgehead in France in 1942, building up ground and air forces there, and expanding the foothold to the limit of our capabilities, changed the character of SLEDGEHAMMER from a 'sacrifice' landing in aid of the Russians to a permanent gain." [100]

ROUNDUP was the code name for the invasion of German-dominated Europe in 1943. Marshall and King apparently altered the original concept of SLEDGEHAMMER to make it more palatable to the British who would have the main burden both in the air and on the ground. In June, Churchill had informed Roosevelt, "We hold strongly to the view that there should be no substantial landing in France this year unless we are going to stay." [101] Before the Americans arrived to make their case, the British chiefs had already concluded that even if landings in France were successful in the autumn, it was not possible to maintain Anglo-American forces there over the winter. Brooke described part of the debate in his diary, "The next argument was that we should take advantage of German preoccupation in Russia to establish a bridgehead for 1943 operations. Had to convince them that there was no hope of such a bridgehead surviving the winter." [102]

The first meeting between Marshall and King and the British chiefs ended without any change of position on either side. The British chiefs, who were unanimously opposed to SLEDGEHAMMER, wanted an Anglo-American invasion of North Africa which had been given the code name GYMNAST. Considerable discussions went on behind the scenes over dinners and well into the evenings. Hopkins spent more time with Churchill than did Marshall and King. On Monday night Brooke noted in his diary that he worked for two hours after dinner and was then sent for by Churchill. When he arrived at 10 Downing Street, he found Hopkins, Harriman, and Beaverbrook. The following night he was again summoned to 10 Downing Street. He arrived there at 11:00 P.M. where he found Hopkins and Eden.

Early in the week Marshall invited Mountbatten to dine with him at Claridge's. The forty-two-year-old British admiral was nineteen years younger than Marshall. Despite this age difference they were very congenial. Marshall had heard that Mountbatten opposed the British stand and wanted to do SLEDGEHAMMER. After the dashing Admiral arrived at Claridge's, standing up in a miniature tank, the two men dined in private. Neither ever revealed anything of their conversation, but it proved to be a futile endeavor for Marshall as Mountbatten never broke ranks with his colleagues.

On Tuesday, at 11:00 A.M., Marshall and King resumed their talks with the British chiefs. While Marshall continued to urge the British to accept SLEDGEHAMMER, he conceded that it could not be commenced before October. Brooke noted in his diary: "Disappointing start. Found ourselves much where we had started yesterday morning except that Marshall admitted that he saw no opportunity of staging an offensive in Europe to assist Russians by September. He missed the point that after September Russians might be past requiring assistance and that weather, at any rate at that season, was such as to make cross-channel operations practically impossible." [103]

Throughout these meetings Marshall had taken the lead. King performed a supportive role. Hopkins did not attend the meetings between the British and American chiefs of staff, but kept in close touch with Marshall and King. In his diary entry for Tuesday Brooke wrote, "We went on arguing for two hours, during which King remained with a face like a Sphinx, and with only one idea, to transfer operations to the Pacific." [104]

After two days of unyielding British opposition to SLEDGE-HAMMER, Hopkins handed either Marshall or King a note on No. 10 Downing Street stationery which read, "I feel damned depressed." [105] He had been a staunch advocate of SLEDGE-HAMMER since the previous March because he saw it as the one sure way to keep Russia in the war.

On Wednesday, July 22, the Combined Chiefs of Staff again met at 11:00 A.M. At the outset the Americans presented the British chiefs with a memorandum advocating an attack on the Cherbourg salient as a preliminary move to a general attack in 1943. In Brooke's opinion, "The memorandum drew attention to the advantages, but failed to recognize the main disadvantage that there was no hope of our still being in Cherbourg by next spring." [106] At the same time Marshall and King informed the British that they would have to report to the president that there was a deadlock on where the first Anglo-American offense against Germany would take place.

Which side was right about SLEDGEHAMMER? The weight of the evidence supports the British. In July of 1942 the Germans had as many as twenty-five divisions in France. The maximum number of divisions that the Allies could land was probably eight. The Cotentin Peninsula was barely within the range of any land-based Allied fighter aircraft. The Luftwaffe would almost certainly have been able to achieve air superiority over the peninsula except for short intervals. Historian John Keegan has concluded that "a cross-channel invasion in 1942 would certainly have ended in catastrophe." [107]

Roosevelt now used his powers as Commander in Chief in a decisive way. He had received information from Hopkins which strengthened his hand. Earlier Hopkins had cabled the president on SLEDGEHAMMER that "Stark is 'lukewarm.'" [108] At the same time that Marshall and King were asking their commander in chief for instructions, Hopkins informed the president that the U.S. Navy officers involved were of the view that the Royal Navy representatives knew what they were about in contending that the weather would preclude a cross-channel operation any later than September.

Sometime in the period of forty-eight hours after he had written out the words, "I feel damned depressed," Hopkins changed his mind about SLEDGEHAMMER. There were at least two factors involved in his decision. He now realized that the British objections had considerable merit. More importantly, he discerned that the president wanted an agreement on an alternative strategy as soon as possible. After learning of the deadlock and Hopkins' information, Roosevelt had cabled his three representatives that "mere acquiescence on the part of our friends is not sufficient." [109]   In this same cable, which was received on Thursday, he instructed Marshall and King to work out an agreement with the British on some other offensive for American ground forces for 1942 with an attack on French North Africa as his first priority. The previous afternoon at 5:30 Churchill put the whole matter to the War Cabinet, who alone could make the final decision to reject SLEDGEHAMMER. All eight members, including Lord Halifax, Ambassador to the United States, were present. Churchill asked each of them to give his views about a cross-channel invasion that year. None could support it.

Notwithstanding any disagreements with the Americans on strategy, the British proceeded to show their guests as much hospitality as wartime conditions allowed. On Wednesday, July 22, Marshall and King dined with the British chiefs. Brooke's diary notes, "This evening Chiefs of Staff gave dinner to Americans at Claridge's. On the whole, went well." [110]

Thursday, July 23, was Alan Brooke's fifty-ninth birthday of which he wrote, " July 23. My birthday—59! I don't feel like it." [111] It would have been understandable had the overburdened British chief taken a few hours that night to dine with his wife. Instead, he invited Marshall to dinner with a small group of his close friends. With some satisfaction Brooke noted in his diary, "Marshall in very pleasant and friendly mood." [112]

That same evening Churchill was the host for a dinner at 10 Downing Street for Admiral King. His mood was anything but "pleasant and friendly." Admiral King's book describes the scene: "The P.M. that evening was extremely morose and generally unpleasant until Mrs. Churchill told him that his chief trouble was that he had to see the Russian Ambassador at ten o'clock the next morning. At this correct diagnosis, Mr. Churchill rose, bowed to his wife and the company, said he was sorry, and instantly became a great deal more agreeable." [113]

At noon on Friday, July 24, Marshall and King presented the British with a new general plan for 1942-1943 on which they and their staffs had spent the better part of two days. Two of its key provisions read:

> (a) That there be no avoidable reduction in the preparation for ROUNDUP as long as there remains any possibility of its successful execution before July 1943; that Allied air strength should be built up in the United Kingdom; that for purposes of deception and for seizing an emergency or a favorable opportunity, all preparations for SLEDGEHAMMER continue except those seriously interfering with ROUNDUP; and that a task force commander be appointed with authority to organize, train and plan for SLEDGEHAMMER.

> (b) That if the Russian situation on 15 September makes ROUNDUP appear impracticable, it be decided to launch combined operations in North Africa at the earliest possible date before December 1942. [114]

The British chiefs made only minor alterations before presenting it to the prime minister and the War Cabinet where it received their approval. Marshall and King understandably thought that the final decision to invade French North Africa had been postponed until September 15. They realized that a cross-channel invasion in 1942 was no longer on the table, but they were still hoping for an invasion of France in 1943.

Churchill and Hopkins were unhappy, however, with any language which made the North African operation contingent on events in Russia. They also worried about the possibility of delay. Using his friend "Pug" Ismay, Hopkins cabled the president through the British Foreign Office. He urged Roosevelt to make the decision to launch the operation now, rather than postponing the decision until September 15. He also strongly recommended a date not later than October 30, 1942 for the invasion itself. His cable was sent to the Foreign Office shortly after noon on Saturday, July 25, with instructions to be delivered to the president immediately wherever he may be. In response, Roosevelt cabled Hopkins, Marshall and King, "Please inform British Chiefs of Staff it is my opinion GYMNAST should be started with landing not later than October 30, 1942." [115]

The largest dinner party for the Americans took place Friday evening, July 24. The Lords of the Admiralty gave it in honor of Admiral King in the painted hall of the Royal Naval College at Greenwich. Around one hundred persons attended the event, including the prime minister, who, King wrote, "added greatly to the geniality of the occasion." [116] The guests were made up of most of the senior officers of the Royal Navy then on duty in London and several senior United States Naval officers including Admiral Stark. Marshall and Eisenhower were invited but had another engagement. "Hopkins attended and enjoyed himself." [117]

Churchill's principal private secretary, John Martin, described the evening in a letter home:

> *I have never seen so many admirals. Their Lordships gave us an excellent dinner after which we went to the young officers' gun-room, where the P.M. toasted Admiral Jacky Fisher's grandson, who was one of them and happened to be celebrating his twenty-first birthday. Alexander, the First Lord, then sat down at the piano and for about an hour thumped out, I should think, every song in the Students' Song Book and conducted community singing with great gusto. The room was crowded with sub-lieutenants, Admirals, and Wrens (who have a training course for officers at Greenwich), all singing at the top of their voices (not excluding the P.M.), the most cheerful party I have seen for a long time. Altogether a memorable evening, which the Americans obviously enjoyed enormously. It ended with Auld Lang Syne and the two national anthems.* [118]

To some this lighthearted occasion in the midst of a desperate war may have seemed unduly frivolous. If so, they were missing a point that was both elementary and sublime. The Americans and the British were able to converse and sing together because they spoke a common language. The English language was in a real sense the symbol of everything else that they had in common.

Saturday, July 25 was the Americans' last full day in England. Before proceeding to Prestwick they stopped off at Chequers for a final dinner with Churchill. Brooke noted in his diary: "Arrived there at 8:00 P.M. Party consisted of P.M., Mrs. Churchill, Marshall, King, Harry Hopkins, Harriman, three Chiefs of Staff, "Pug," Martin and Tommy (Commander Thompson). After dinner the Americans were shown Cromwell's death mask and Queen Elizabeth's ring. They then left by special train for Scotland to fly to America." [119]

The Chief of the Imperial General Staff for one was greatly relieved with the outcome of the London Conference. The previous night he had written, "A very trying week, but it is satisfactory to feel that we have got just what we wanted out of U.S. Chiefs." [120] Churchill too was much relieved. He would write after the war, "All was therefore agreed and settled in accordance with my long-conceived ideas and those of my colleagues, military and political. This was a great joy to me, especially as it came in what seemed to be the darkest hour." [121]

Of the three Americans whom Roosevelt had sent to London, Harry Hopkins was the only one to receive Churchill's praise. On July 27 Churchill opened his cable to Roosevelt with these words: "I was sure you would be pleased as I am, indeed as we all are here, at the results of this strenuous week. Besides reaching complete agreement on action, relations of cordial intimacy, and comradeship have been cemented between our high officers. I doubt if success would have been achieved without Harry's invaluable aid." [122]

This raises an unanswered, historical query. What exactly was "Harry's invaluable aid?" Although Churchill did not elaborate, it was clear that Hopkins had contributed to the successful resolution of what John Keegan has called "perhaps the hardest-fought strategic debate in the war." [123] For three days Marshall had argued adamantly for SLEDGEHAMMER and against GYMNAST. He saw the North African operation as a misguided diversion of American forces from the vital theatre. If SLEDGEHAMMER was out of the question, then what he wanted most was a buildup of men and supplies in the British Isles in preparation for a cross-channel invasion in 1943. He realized that the size and scope of the North African operation would make it impossible to carry out ROUNDUP the following year.

While there may be no direct evidence, the circumstances indicate that Hopkins influenced Marshall's decision to accept,

subject to conditions, the British view. In 1957 Marshall spoke
to Pogue of his relations with Hopkins:

> I think you have Hopkins pretty well pegged, but I will
> say this: he was invaluable to me. I didn't see Hopkins
> very often because I made it my business not to go to the
> White House, but the others, like Arnold and Somervell,
> would see him with great frequency. But whenever I hit a
> tough knot I couldn't handle and seemingly couldn't get
> anywhere, I would call him up and he would either arrange
> the meeting with the President for me, or he and I together
> would see the President. And we had a number of talks
> with the President with no one else present. He was
> always the strong advocate, it seemed to me, of almost
> everything I proposed, and it required quite a bit of expla-
> nation from time to time to have the President see that the
> setup could not be handled in the ways he sometimes sug-
> gested. And there had to be a very firm position taken in
> these matters. So he was quite invaluable to me and he
> was very courageous. [124]

In London, Hopkins' role was reversed. There he acted as
Roosevelt's advocate to convince Marshall that above all the
president wanted to preserve unity with "our friends" and that
the time had come to back an offensive operation acceptable to
them. It is hard not to conclude that this was the reason that
Churchill had cabled Roosevelt, "I doubt if success would have
been achieved without Harry's invaluable aid."

Harry Hopkins returned to America in a state of euphoria
which had nothing to do with the decision to invade North
Africa, the code name for which had been changed from GYM-
NAST to TORCH. He was about to be married to Louise Macy.
Their wedding took place at noon on Thursday, July 30, 1942 in
the Oval Study on the second floor of the White House.
Reverend Russell Clinchy of Hartford, Connecticut conducted
the service. Hopkins' sons, David, Robert and Stephen, and his
daughter, Diana, who turned ten that year, were all there. The
guests included the President & Mrs. Roosevelt, General
Marshall and Admiral King. Of Hopkins' many homecomings
during the war this was certainly one of his happiest.

The drama over the issue of TORCH did not end after the
London Conference. Shortly after returning to Washington,
General Marshall made one last attempt to block TORCH or to
delay a final decision. He was overruled by the commander in
chief. It was perhaps the only time during the war that

The wedding of Harry L. Hopkins and Louise Macy at the White House on July 30, 1942. The guests included President and Mrs. Roosevelt; Hopkins's sons, David (behind the children), Robert (in his army uniform), and Stephen (on Robert's left; his daughter, Diana (next to the president); his wife's sister, Mrs. Nicholas Ludington (on the far right of the Hopkinses) and his wife's brother-in-law, Lt. Nicholas Ludington U.S.N. (on the far left of the Hopkinses).

President Roosevelt ordered a major military operation against the advice of the Joint Chiefs. Concerning this conflict Robert E. Sherwood would later write:

> At the end of July, after Hopkins had left Washington for his honeymoon, the Joint Chiefs of Staff unanimously recommended against the North African landings, but the President summoned them to the White House to inform them that the decision to undertake the TORCH operation as early as possible must be carried out. He insisted that preparations for the landings must be pushed forward rapidly and vigorously. [125]

The White House meeting to which Sherwood refers could only have occurred in the evening of July 30. Following the Hopkins' wedding Roosevelt had a full schedule for the remainder of the afternoon. The next day both he and General Marshall were outside of Washington. The president was at Hyde Park and the general was at Leesburg. On the day of Hopkins' wedding the Joint Chiefs had been expanded to include Admiral William D. Leahy who would serve as the president's representative on that group. From July 30, 1942, Admiral Leahy, as the senior officer, presided over all meetings of the Joint Chiefs. It is virtually certain that both Admiral Leahy and General Marshall were at the White House on the evening of July 30. Admiral King and General Arnold, the Air Chief of Staff, were also probably there. No minutes were kept. Of the five participants three would write books about the war years. King chose not to mention the conflict with the president over the North African invasion. Arnold described it discreetly in twenty words. "It was the President himself, with the Prime Minister, who decided to make this gigantic diversion, TORCH, our first priority." [126]

Leahy was somewhat more explicit. He wrote, "It has been said that Roosevelt ordered 'Operation TORCH' in the face of opposition of his senior advisers. I never opposed the North African invasion. I told the President of the possibilities of trouble, but it looked to me like a feasible undertaking. Marshall did oppose it. He did not want to waste American troops in North Africa when he thought he could use them in a cross-channel operation." [127]

What was Hopkins' involvement in Roosevelt's decision to overrule a majority of the Joint Chiefs? While there is no definitive answer, the circumstances suggest that Hopkins was deeply

involved in the process by which the president reached his decision. Hopkins had spent considerably more time with Churchill
than had either Marshall or King. He would have certainly
apprised the president of Churchill's reasons for favoring an
invasion of North Africa. He would also have given Roosevelt his
own opinion which would have undergirded the president's defi-
nite inclination.

After his return to Washington Hopkins continued to reside
at the White House where he was in closer contact with
Roosevelt than anyone else. It can only be assumed that when
Harry Hopkins left Washington on July 30 for his honeymoon,
he did so with the satisfaction of knowing that at long last the
president had made a final decision to launch the initial Anglo-
American offensive against Nazi Germany regardless of any
objections from the Joint Chiefs. Other than the Normandy
landings it was perhaps the single most important decision of
the war.

PART IV

THE FINAL MISSION

Harry Truman arose at dawn. It was Saturday, April 14, 1945. He had been president of the United States for less than thirty-six hours. He felt overwhelmed by the burden of his office and feared that he lacked the ability to be president. Most historians agree that he was singularly ill-prepared to assume his new responsibilities. During Truman's vice-presidency of less than three months, Roosevelt had failed to inform him about the development of the atomic bomb, the understandings reached with Stalin and Churchill at Yalta, or Roosevelt's plans for America's role in the postwar world.

If Truman was unfamiliar with foreign policy issues, he was also unfamiliar with the two key players on the world stage. He had never met Churchill or Stalin. Roosevelt's closest foreign policy adviser had been neither Cordell Hull, his long-suffering secretary of state, nor Hull's successor, Edward R. Stettinius, Jr., who lacked diplomatic experience. Before the United States entered the war, President Roosevelt had used Harry L. Hopkins as his personal envoy for diplomatic missions at the highest levels. For most of the war Hopkins was one of the most powerful individuals in Washington because of his access to the president who sought his advice on almost all matters of importance. When Roosevelt met Churchill and Stalin at Yalta in February 1945, Hopkins was unquestionably his closest foreign policy adviser.

Fortunately for the country, the new president and Hopkins knew one another. Their acquaintance went back to 1934 when Hopkins ran the W.P.A. and Truman was director of the Federal Reemployment Service in Missouri. Their relationship, however, did not flourish until Truman became a United States senator in 1935. Truman was then age fifty, knew almost no one in Washington, and was without any experience as a legislator. Afterwards, Truman "would fondly recall Harry Hopkins...because Hopkins had shown him kindness in this most difficult of times..." [128]

On that first Saturday as President Truman went to Washington's Union Station where he boarded the train that had

brought Franklin Roosevelt's body back to the Capitol from
Warm Springs. After paying his respects to Mrs. Roosevelt he
rode in the cortege that slowly wound its way back to the White
House through streets lined with mourners. His first appoint-
ment on returning to the White House was with Harry Hopkins.
Truman had requested this meeting as soon as he had learned
that Hopkins had returned to Washington from the Mayo Clinic
where he had spent over two months following the Yalta
Conference. Hopkins was still far from well. Truman would
long remember his friend's appearance on that solemn day.
"...when he entered my office this time, he looked worse than
ever before. He was ill, of course, and the death of Roosevelt
had affected him profoundly. If I had not known his great patri-
otism and his spirit of self-sacrifice, I would have hesitated to
tax his strength." [129]

Their discussion on April 14 was the first of several meetings
which the two men had in April and early May. Truman sought
Hopkins' advice, primarily regarding problems with Russia. The
most difficult of these problems concerned Russian intentions
toward Poland. On May 4, Truman for the first time suggested
to Hopkins the possibility of sending him to see Stalin. Hopkins
demurred on the ground that he needed to talk to his doctor
before reaching any decision on such a lengthy journey. By
coincidence, Averell Harriman, the American ambassador to
Russia, and Charles E. Bohlen, the State Department's liaison
officer with the White House, were thinking along the same line.
On May 9, while returning by plane to Washington from the
organizational meeting of the United Nations in San Francisco,
the two men had a long discussion about what could be done to
restore Soviet-American relations. Bohlen broached the possibility of a Hopkins mission. Harriman was receptive and when
they approached Hopkins at his Georgetown home, he put aside
his health concerns and eagerly embraced the idea. Based on
the recommendation of Bohlen, Harriman, and Cordell Hull, but
against the advice of James F. Byrnes, who would soon replace
Stettinius as secretary of state, Truman once again asked
Hopkins to meet with Stalin. Hopkins immediately accepted.

It was now apparent to Truman that Russian behavior
toward Poland was contrary to the understandings reached at
Yalta. Within two weeks of Roosevelt's death Truman had been
informed by Stettinius that there was a complete deadlock on
the subject of carrying out the Yalta agreement on Poland.
Stettinius had emphasized to the new president "that the Lublin
or Warsaw government was not representative of the Polish people and that it was now clear that the Russians intended to try

to force this puppet government upon the United States and England." [130]

On May 12 Truman received an ominous warning from Churchill which read in part, "I am profoundly concerned about the European situation...I feel deep anxiety because of (Russian) misinterpretations of the Yalta decisions, their attitudes toward Poland...and above all their power to maintain very large armies in the field for a long time...An iron curtain is drawn down upon their front. We do not know what is going on behind." [131] It was almost a year before Churchill's speech at Fulton, Missouri, where he would make the historic declaration, "From Stettin in the Baltic to Trieste in the Adriatic, an iron curtain has descended across the Continent." [132]

In the face of an impending crisis and with a meeting with Churchill and Stalin in the offing, Truman felt that it was imperative that he know whether Roosevelt's death had caused any important changes in Stalin's attitude toward Russian commitments at Yalta. Truman was determined to hold the Soviet government to all of its agreements. In his final instructions to Hopkins, he told him "that in talking to Stalin he was free to use diplomatic language or a baseball bat if he thought that was the proper approach." [133]

Hopkins asked his friend Bohlen to accompany him. The two had become friends at the Cairo Conference where Hopkins "had asked him all manner of questions about the Soviet Union and was surprised and impressed by the objectivity and lack of bias as well as the considerable scholarship revealed in his answers." [134] Bohlen, who was fluent in the Russian language, would have the responsibility of interpreting every word that Hopkins said to Stalin.

Hopkins, his wife Louise, and Bohlen flew out of Washington's National Airport on May 23 bound for Paris where they were joined by Harriman who had been in London briefing Churchill on Hopkins' mission. From there they flew across Germany to Moscow. One historian has asserted that "Hopkins was not briefed on Polish affairs." [135] In the broad sense this statement is unfounded. President Truman, who had quickly grasped the rudiments of the Polish problem, had met with Hopkins at least three times. Hopkins, Harriman, and Bohlen had all been at Yalta where Poland was discussed "at no fewer than seven out of the eight plenary meetings." [136] Not only was Harriman the United States ambassador to Russia, he, along with V. M. Molotov and Sir A. Clark Kerr, had been appointed to a commission to prepare a joint recommendation concerning a reorganized Polish Provisional government which was more broadly based than the Warsaw government created by Moscow.

The vital issue facing Hopkins was whether Stalin would live up to his Yalta pledge to permit free, multi-party elections in Poland. There were other unresolved conflicts with the Russians over Poland. Sixteen leaders of the Polish underground had disappeared without a trace on March 27. The Russians belatedly admitted having arrested them. The United States and Britain were demanding their release. The immediate issue was the lack of any agreement on the selection of those individuals who would be invited to Moscow to consult with the commission and the representatives of the Warsaw government on an enlarged Polish Provisional government.

The first of six meetings with Stalin commenced in the Kremlin at 8:00 P.M. on May 25, 1945. Present were Stalin, Molotov, Pavlov (Stalin's interpreter), Hopkins, Harriman, and Bohlen. Among the Americans only Bohlen spoke fluent Russian. Stalin was acquainted with all of the Americans, but Hopkins was the one to whom he could best relate. Once in Bohlen's presence Stalin had said that "Hopkins was the first American to whom he had spoken 'po dushe'—from the soul." [137] Bohlen recalled in his memoirs that "Stalin certainly went out of his way to be extremely courteous to Hopkins." [138] Hopkins knew that he was dealing with a tough Russian who always thought first and foremost of Russia, but, at least at the outset, he thought that Stalin could be talked to frankly.

Hopkins opened the meeting with a light reference to Molotov's recent visit to the United States. He asked the commissar whether he had recovered from the battle of San Francisco. The humorless Molotov replied that he could not recall any battles, but merely arguments. Hopkins then proceeded to give Stalin his thoughts about Roosevelt's state of mind after the conclusion of the Yalta Conference. He told Stalin that Roosevelt "had come away from that conference with renewed confidence that the United States and the Soviet Union could work together in peace as they had in war." [139] It was hardly surprising that Hopkins' first remarks to Stalin evoked the late president. Hopkins revered Roosevelt and believed that Stalin and the Russian people perhaps felt a debt of gratitude to him for his help during the war.

Hopkins gradually led the discussion toward Poland by describing the changes of American public opinion toward Russia that had occurred in the last six weeks. He reminded Stalin that it had been a cardinal basis of President Roosevelt's policy fully supported by the American people that the interests of the United States were worldwide and not confined to North and South America and the Pacific. Hopkins then confronted

Courtesy of the Harry S. Truman Library

Hopkins discusses his Moscow meetings with President Truman, former Ambassador to Russia Joseph E. Davies and Presidential Chief of Staff Fleet Admiral William D. Leahy at the White House on June 13, 1945.

Stalin with the pivotal issue. He stated that the deterioration in public opinion "had been centered in our inability to carry into effect the Yalta Agreement on Poland." [140]

Stalin immediately blamed the British, stating, "the reason for the failure of the Polish question was that the Soviet Union desired to have a friendly Poland, but that Great Britain wanted to revive the system of cordon sanitaire on the Soviet borders." [141] Hopkins replied that "neither the government nor the people of the United States had any such intention." [142] Hopkins clearly wanted Stalin to know how strongly he felt about the Polish issue. He told Stalin "he had wished to state frankly and as forcibly as he knew how to Marshal Stalin the importance that he, personally, attached to the present trend of events and that he felt that the situation would get rapidly worse unless we could clear up the Polish matter." [143]

The second meeting involving the same individuals commenced at 8:00 P.M. on May 27. Hopkins opened the meeting by inviting Stalin to raise any matters involving the United States that worried him. The Russian leader responded by complaining about the American decision that Argentina should be invited to the organizational conference of the United Nations at San

Francisco, about the inclusion of France on the War Reparations Commission, which he said was an insult to the Soviet Union, about the manner in which Lend Lease had been curtailed, and about the disposition of the German Navy and merchant fleet. On the question of Poland he was hard and unyielding, telling Hopkins that what had been agreed at Yalta was to reconstruct the existing government and "that anyone with common sense could see that this meant that the present government was to form the basis of the new. He said no other understanding of the Yalta Agreement was possible." [144] Hopkins and his two colleagues were well aware that the "present government" was totally subservient to the Soviet Union.

Hopkins allayed Stalin's concerns over non-Polish matters and proceeded to place the Polish problem in the context of Soviet-American relations telling Stalin that "the question of Poland per se was not so important as the fact that it had become a symbol of our ability to work out problems with the Soviet Union." [145] He went on to tell Stalin that the people and the government of the United States "felt that the Polish people should be given the right to free elections to choose their own government and their own system and that Poland should be genuinely independent." [146]

Stalin responded, saying that previous European policies had allowed a weak and unfriendly Poland to serve as a corridor for two German invasions of Russia. He stressed that it was in Russia's vital interests that the nation of Poland be both strong and friendly. He disclaimed any intention on the part of the Soviet Union to interfere in the internal affairs of Poland. He even ventured the prediction that Poland would live under a parliamentary system comparable to Czechoslovakia, Belgium, and Holland. To make his point unmistakably clear to the Americans he told them, "any talk of an intention to Sovietize Poland was stupid." [147] According to Stalin, even the Polish communist leaders were against the Soviet system and they were right because the Soviet system was not exportable. He justified his government's unilateral action in recognizing the Warsaw government and in concluding a treaty with it on the grounds that the security of the Red Army demanded that its rear areas be protected and that the Warsaw government's predecessor, the so-called Lublin Committee, had been of great assistance in this regard.

At this point, Stalin made what seemed at the time an important concession. He informed Hopkins that Stanislaw Mikolajczyk, whom he had previously rejected as a participant in any discussions concerning a reorganized Polish Provisional government, was now acceptable. Earlier, Churchill had informed Stalin that Mikolajczyk was "considered throughout Britain and America as the outstanding Polish figure abroad." [148] In the course of events, Mikolajczyk participated in the discussions and subsequently became a second deputy premier and minister of agriculture and land reform in the communist-dominated Provisional government. However, in 1947 he fled to England when a Stalinist takeover became a reality.

Hopkins requested some time to consider Stalin's suggestions. After each meeting Hopkins cabled President Truman and the State Department a comprehensive report.

Stalin's attitude toward Poland during his meetings with Hopkins reflected more than concern about the possible resurgence of German aggression. Judged by his deeds, rather than his words, Stalin considered non-communist Poles enemies who deserved the cruelest kind of treatment. His more odious deeds included an unprovoked attack on Poland, the mass-murder of Polish officers, and a cold-blooded decision to allow the Germans to suppress the 1944 Warsaw uprising. Stalin launched his invasion of Poland on September 17, 1939, after the bulk of the Polish Army had already been crushed by the Wehrmacht. Some 14,700 Police Army Officers were among those detained by the Red Army in concentration camps near the Katyn Forest in eastern Poland. After April 1940 no further word of their whereabouts was heard by the Polish government-in-exile.

Although the German Army overran the Katyn Forest in the summer of 1941, it was not until April 1943 that the Germans discovered mass graves in that area. With considerable fanfare the Germans publicly charged the Soviets with the murder of the Polish officers. Moscow denied any involvement and accused the Germans of the massacre. When the London-based Polish government-in-exile demanded an impartial investigation by the International Red Cross, Stalin broke off relations with them. No impartial investigation was ever conducted. Russia's allies wanted to believe that Germany was the guilty party, but most Poles thought otherwise. For decades the facts about the Katyn Forest massacre remained obscure. Finally, in 1994, Russian archivists uncovered a letter dated March 5, 1940, to Comrade Stalin from the People's Commissar for Internal Affairs of the USSR, L. Beria. It reads in part:

> In view of the fact that all are hardened and uncompromising enemies of the Soviet authority, the USSR NKVD considers it necessary...that it should try before special tribunals 1) the cases of the 14,700 former Polish officers,

government officials, landowners, police officers, intelli-
gence officers, gendarmes, settlers in border regions, and
prison guards being kept in prisoner-of-war camps. 2) and
also the cases of 11,000 members of various counterrevolu-
tionary organizations...and apply to them the supreme
penalty: shooting. [149]

This letter was endorsed for action by Stalin's signature. In all, 25,700 Poles were murdered at Stalin's direction in the Katyn Forest.

The Warsaw uprising began on August 1, 1944, after Soviet broadcasting stations had urged "the Polish population to drop all caution and start a general revolt against the Germans." [150] The Red Army had by then advanced to the Vistula River just east of Warsaw, but acting under orders, it failed to render any meaningful support to the Poles. Stalin refused to allow American or British planes to land on Soviet airfields for refueling after their long and dangerous flights over Warsaw to drop supplies to the Polish fighters. During the height of the battle Stalin cabled Churchill, "sooner or later the truth about the group of criminals who have embarked on the Warsaw adventure in order to seize power will become known to everybody." [151]

The battle for Warsaw daily became more desperate. The lightly armed Poles were systematically wiped out by German forces equipped with heavy armor. The Polish Underground Army lost fifteen thousand killed-in-action. Polish civilian casualties amounted to nearly two hundred thousand deaths. Churchill would devote a full chapter in his final volume on the Second World War to "the Martyrdom of Warsaw" which concluded with these words: "When the Russians entered the city three months later they found little but shattered streets and the unburied dead. Such was their liberation of Poland, where they now rule. But this cannot be the end of the story." [152]

Hopkins could not have had any illusions about Stalin's past deeds except for the Katyn Forest massacre which Hopkins probably then thought was the work of Hitler.

When Hopkins returned to Spaso House, the Ambassador's residence, following his second meeting with Stalin, he summoned George F. Kennan, who was chargé d'affaires in Harriman's absence. Unknown to anyone in the United States government with the exception of Harriman, Kennan had produced two insightful analyses of Soviet leadership and Soviet policy toward eastern Europe. In a private memorandum prepared in September 1944 called, "Russia—Seven Years Later," Kennan had written:

It would be useful to the Western World to realize that
despite all the vicissitudes by which Russia had been
afflicted since August 1939, the men in the Kremlin have
never abandoned their faith in that program of territorial
and political expansion which had once commended itself
so strongly to Tsarist diplomatists and which underlay the
German-Russian Nonaggression Pact of 1939. The program meant the reestablishment of Russian power in
Finland and the Baltic states, in eastern Poland, in northern Bukovina, and in Bessarabia. It meant a protectorate
over western Poland and an access to the sea from the
Russian Empire somewhere in East Prussia...Joseph
Vissarionovich Stalin, now in the sixty-fifth year of his
life and the twentieth year of his power in Russia, is the
most powerful and the least known of the world's leaders...Courageous but wary; quick to anger and suspicion
but patient and persistent in the execution of his purposes;
capable of acting with great decision or of waiting and dis-
sembling, as circumstances may require; outwardly modest
and simple, but jealous of the prestige and dignity of the
state which he leads; not learned, yet shrewd and pitiless-
ly realistic; exacting in his demands for loyalty, respect
and obedience; a keen and unsentimental student of men—
he can be, like a true Georgian hero, a great and good
friend or an implacable, dangerous enemy. [153]

Only a few weeks before Hopkins' arrival Kennan completed a
second memorandum, entitled "Russia's International Position
at the close of the War with Germany." This document included
the following passage:

All in all, therefore, it can be seen that Russia will not
have an easy time in maintaining the power which it has
seized over other people in Eastern and Central Europe
unless it receives both moral and material assistance from
the West. It must therefore be Russian policy in the coming
period to persuade the Western nations, and particularly
the United States (1) to give its blessing to Russian domina-
tion of these areas by recognizing Russian puppet states as
independent countries and dealing with them as such, thus
collaborating with the Soviet government in maintaining the
fiction by which these countries are ruled; and (2) to grant
to Russia the extensive material support which would
enable the Soviet government to make good the economic
damages caused by its costly and uncompromising political

*program and to claim credit for bringing economic as well
as political progress to the peoples in question.* [154]

As tired as he was that night, Hopkins would have been
enormously interested in each memorandum. It is possible that
Hopkins read the more recent one. In his memoirs Kennan
noted, "A faint prompting of memory suggests to me that it may
have been read by Harry Hopkins, when he visited Moscow in
that same month of 1945." [155] Hopkins apparently made no
record of their meeting that night. Kennan's account best
speaks for itself:

> *My last responsible encounter with the Polish problem
> occurred when shortly after Franklin Roosevelt's death,
> Harry Hopkins, himself with only a few weeks [sic] to live,
> visited Moscow to see what could be salvaged from the
> wreckage of FDR's policy with relation to Russia and
> Poland.*
>
> *At some point during his visit, after at least the first—
> and I believe the second as well—of his interviews with
> Stalin, Hopkins summoned me to Spaso House to inquire
> my opinion. I was amazed at this. I did not know him
> well. I had not been kept informed about his dealings with
> Stalin; and I had not expected to be consulted on these
> matters. He described to me Stalin's terms for a settlement
> of the Polish problem, as developed in his talks at the
> Kremlin and asked whether I thought we could do any bet-
> ter. I said I did not. Did I think, then, that we should
> accept these terms and come to an agreement on this
> basis? I did not; I thought we should accept no share of the
> responsibility for what the Russians proposed to do in
> Poland.*
>
> *"Then you think it's just sin," he said, "and we should
> be agin it." "That's just about right," I replied. "I respect
> your opinion," he said sadly. "But I am not at liberty to
> accept it."* [156]

While Hopkins now had serious doubt that Stalin would
allow free elections in Poland, he was not ready to concede the
issue. At his third meeting with Stalin he made no attempt to
reopen the debate over Poland; however, on May 30 at their
fourth meeting, Hopkins made a valiant attempt to convince
Stalin that a parliamentary government in Poland could not sur-
vive without basic freedoms.

Hopkins said he would like to accent once again the reason for our concern in regard to Poland, and, indeed, in regard to other countries which were geographically far from our borders. He said there were certain fundamental rights which, when impinged upon or denied, caused concern in the United States. These were cardinal elements which must be present if a parliamentary system is to be established and maintained. He said for example:

1. There must be the right of freedom of speech so that people could say what they wanted to, right of assembly, right of movement and the right to worship at any church that they desired;

2. All political parties except the fascist party and fascist elements who represented or could represent democratic governments should be permitted the free use, without distinction, of the press, radio, meetings and other facilities of political expression.

3. All citizens should have the right of public trial, defense by counsel of their own choosing, and the right of habeas corpus. [157]

Even Stalin could not ignore the poignancy of Hopkins' words. His response was as shrewd as it was disingenuous. Stalin told Hopkins that the Soviet government had no objection to those principles of democracy and that the Polish government would welcome them. His only reservations regarding the political freedoms that Hopkins had mentioned were that they could not be enjoyed to the full extent in time of war and they could not be applied to fascists trying to overthrow a government. In conclusion, Stalin told Hopkins "that the present war had wiped out (the) antagonism (with the Russian Orthodox Church) and that now the freedom of religion, as promised, could be granted to the church." [158] That night Hopkins sent Truman a top secret cable which read in part:

I completed the exposition of your position relative to Poland with Stalin. The conference tonight was encouraging. It looks as though Stalin is prepared to return to and implement the Crimea decision and permit a representative group of Poles to come to Moscow to consult with the Commission. [159]

At the fifth meeting between Hopkins and Stalin, on May 31, they focused on the names of various candidates to consult with the Commission on the reorganized Polish government. Stalin insisted that aside from the representatives of the Warsaw government, only three Poles from London and five Poles from Poland could be involved in the consultations. Stalin accepted two out of three proposed candidates from London and three of five proposed candidates from Poland. Later that night, Hopkins cabled the president recommending that he approve the eight individuals on whom they had agreed and that he urge Churchill to do the same.

The next evening Stalin gave a dinner party in Hopkins' honor. Mikoyan, Beria, and Malenkov were among these in attendance. In a private meeting after dinner Hopkins told Stalin that the detention of the sixteen Polish leaders was having an unfavorable effect in America because most of them were merely charged with having illegal radio transmitters. Hopkins then reminded Stalin of the many ethnic groups in America who were not sympathetic to the Soviet Union. Stalin responded that he was unwilling to order the release of any of the Polish leaders prior to their trials. He accused Churchill of misleading the United States regarding the facts of these cases and again blamed Britain for the impasse over Poland saying "that he did not intend to have the British manage the affairs of Poland..." [160]

For the next few days Hopkins relaxed and awaited further instructions from the White House. Prior to his sixth and final meeting with Stalin on June 6, Hopkins received an urgent message from Truman to press Stalin to drop the Russian insistence that each permanent member of the Security Council hold a veto over the subject of discussions by that body. The position of the United States and Britain was that the veto power could only be exercised with respect to enforcement actions in any of its aspects. This dispute threatened to wreck the United Nations organizational meeting. Hopkins ably presented the American case and notwithstanding Molotov's objections, "...Stalin then stated that he was prepared to accept the American position on the point at issue at San Francisco in regard to voting procedure." [161]

Hopkins' achievement did not go unnoticed by Edward Frederick Lindley Wood, First Earl of Halifax. The British ambassador was a member of the British delegation at the San Francisco conference. Halifax, a devout Anglican, had served his country as Viceroy of India, foreign secretary and for over four years as ambassador in Washington. Despite his aristocratic, upperclass background, Roosevelt and Hopkins had grown to admire him for his rectitude and his intellect. Ten years after the war he published his memoirs, *Fullness of Days,* dedicated to his wife, Dorothy, who had been of invaluable assistance to him with all manner of Americans. One of its most memorable passages concerns Hopkins' role in resolving the most serious crisis of the San Francisco Conference.

> ...more than once the fate of the future organization seemed to hang uncertainly in the balance...The Soviet representative Gromyko,...received every argument and appeal with a simple repetition of the formula "The Soviet Government do not agree"...finally we adjourned for luncheon, at which it so happened we were all to be guests of the Soviet delegation.
>
> I found myself sitting next to Gromyko, and as we sat down told him that I could hardly have believed any government could have given its representative instructions to behave in a fashion so unreasoning, unreasonable and intolerable as those on which he had evidently been acting all the morning; but, I added, I now understood how it was that his countrymen had managed to hold Stalingrad against apparently hopeless odds. This observation was received with long and loud laughter and our luncheon was easy. Still it did not get us any closer to a solution to our morning difference. For this we had to appeal to Harry Hopkins who, though already a dying man, had with great gallantry agreed at the request of President Truman to go to Moscow on the Polish business, and it was thanks to him that the United Nations project was able to surmount what looked like being a fatal obstacle. [162]

At the conclusion of their final meeting Hopkins asked Stalin to allow three representatives of the American Red Cross to supervise the distribution of medical supplies in Poland. Stalin said that while he had no objection, it would be necessary to obtain the opinion of the Polish Provisional government. Thus the Hopkins mission came to an end with a pointed reminder that, for at least the immediate future, the United States would be forced to deal with the Polish government that the Soviets had created.

These unprecedented meetings with Stalin failed to save Poland from four decades of communist rule during which the fundamental freedoms that meant so much to Hopkins were conspicuously absent, but it is hard to believe that anyone could have obtained a genuine commitment from Stalin to allow free elections in that country.

Did these meetings with Stalin affect Hopkins' thinking on the future of Soviet-American relations? In the post-Yalta euphoria Hopkins had told Robert Sherwood, "We really believed in our hearts that this was the dawn of the new day we had all been praying for and talking about for so many years. We were absolutely certain that we had won the first great victory of the peace and by 'we' I mean all of us, the whole civilized human race...We felt sure that we could count on (Stalin) to be reasonable and sensible and understanding—but we never could be sure who or what might be back of him there in the Kremlin." 163

During their journey back to the United States Hopkins and Bohlen had long discussions. Bohlen's opinion of Stalin was based on over ten years of experience beginning with his arrival at the Moscow train station on March 8, 1934, as a thirty-year-old career foreign service officer. In his memoirs, Bohlen raised the question, "whether Stalin was simply a realist with no moral values or a monster whose paranoia led him into senseless crimes." 164 Bohlen was convinced that Stalin was the latter.

Concerning his discussions with Hopkins after Moscow, Bohlen would write, "Hopkins, in private talks with me, began to voice for the first time serious doubts as to the possibility of genuine collaboration with the Soviet Union saying he thought our relations were going to be stormy. He based his views primarily on the absence of freedom in the Soviet Union." 165 Hopkins' thinking was clearly more in line with Bohlen's than it had been only four months before when the two men had returned home together from Yalta. These two friends, however, would always perceive the Soviet Union in different lights. Bohlen worried more than Hopkins about the Soviet threat to Western Europe. Hopkins would always hold "one central idea, that good relations between the United States, the Soviet Union, and Great Britain were the most important factor in the world and that everything should be done to promote them." 166

EPILOGUE

Harry Hopkins would never undertake another mission for his country. He hoped that a long rest and good medical care would restore his health. He also hoped to write at least two books, the first on the war and the second on Roosevelt as he knew him. Neither hope was realized. A week before his death on January 29, 1946, Hopkins wrote Churchill, "I am getting excellent care, while the doctors are struggling over a very bad case of cirrhosis of the liver—not due, I regret to say, from taking too much alcohol." [167] The real cause of his death was a disease called hemochromatosis, the result of his inadequate digestive system.

If the final period of his life was far less productive and far shorter than he had wished, it was not without honors. By letter dated June 19, 1945, Oxford University notified Hopkins that "the Hebdomadal Council desires, subject to your consent, to submit to the Convocation of the University at an early date a proposal that the Honorary Degree of D.C.L. be conferred upon you in recognition of your eminent services to the Allied cause." [168] On September 4, 1945, Harry Hopkins was received at the White House. For three and one-half years he had resided there as Roosevelt's guest. Now he stood in the Rose Garden surrounded by family to receive the Distinguished Service Medal. President Truman greeted him as an old friend, presented the medal, and read the full text of the War Department Citation which concluded:

> At major conferences of world powers he threw his every effort toward the speedy solution of weighty problems. With deep appreciation of the armed forces' needs and broad understanding of the Commander-in-Chief's overall policy, with exceptional ability to weld our Allies to the common purpose of victory over aggression, Mr. Hopkins made a selfless, courageous and objective contribution to the war effort. [169]

NOTES

1. Martin Gilbert, *Finest Hour Winston S. Churchill 1939 1941* (London: Heinemann-Minerva, 1989), 694.

2. Peter Collier and David Horowitz, *The Kennedys: An American Drama* (New York: Summit Books, 1984), 106.

3. William Stevenson, *A Man Called Intrepid* (New York: Harcourt Brace Jovanovich, 1976), 149-50.

4. Charles A. Lindbergh, *The Wartime Journals of Charles A. Lindbergh* (New York: Harcourt Brace Jovanovich, 1970), 420.

5. Arthur M. Schlesinger, Jr., *The Politics of Upheaval* (Boston: Houghton Mifflin, 1960), 356.

6. Robert E. Sherwood, *Roosevelt and Hopkins: An Intimate History* (New York: Harper Brothers, 1948), 120.

7. Ibid., 121.

8. Ibid., 238.

9. Ibid.

10. John Colville, *The Fringes of Power* (New York: W. W. Norton Company, 1985) 331.

11. Ibid., 332.

12. Ibid., 333.

13. Sherwood, *Roosevelt and Hopkins*, 243.

14. *The King James Bible*, Psalms, Chapter 107, verse 23.

15. Lord Moran, *Churchill Taken from the Diaries of Lord Moran* (Boston: Houghton Mifflin, 1966), 6.

16. Gilbert, *Finest Hour*, 992.

17. Sherwood, *Roosevelt and Hopkins*, 241

18. Ibid., 248-49.

19. Colville, *The Fringes of Power*, 341.

20. Ibid.

21. Ibid., 345-47.

22. Gilbert, *Finest Hour*, 999.

23. George McJimsey, *Harry Hopkins, Ally of the Poor and Defender of Democracy*, (Cambridge: Harvard University Press, 1987), 148.

24. David Cannadine, ed., *Blood, Toil, Tears and Sweat, The Speeches of Winston Churchill* (Boston: Houghton Mifflin, 1989), 213.

25. Moran, *Churchill Taken From the Diaries of Lord Moran*, 6.

26. Sherwood, *Roosevelt and Hopkins*, 250.

27. Colville, *The Fringes of Power*, 355.

28. Pamela Churchill Harriman, remarks made by her at the opening of the private papers of Harry L. Hopkins at Georgetown University on January 26, 1986.

29. Winston S. Churchill, *The Grand Alliance* (Boston: Houghton Mifflin Company, 1950), 128.

30. Ibid.

31. Gilbert, *Finest Hour*, 1022.

32. Sherwood, *Roosevelt and Hopkins*, 806.

33. Martin Gilbert, *Winston S. Churchill, Volume VII, Road to Victory 1941-1945* (Boston: Houghton Mifflin Company, 1986), 1086.

34. Dan van der Vat, *The Atlantic Campaign* (New York: Harper and Row, 1988), 233.

35. Henry H. Adams, *Harry Hopkins: A Biography* (New York: G. P. Putnam's Sons, 1977), 368.

36. Winston S. Churchill, *Triumph and Tragedy* (Boston: Houghton Mifflin Company, 1953), 397.

37. Ibid., 472.

38. Charles E. Bohlen, *Witness to History* (New York: W. W. Norton, 1973), 239.

39. McJimsey, *Harry Hopkins*, 393.

40. Sherwood, *Roosevelt and Hopkins*, 931.

41. Churchill, *The Grand Alliance*, 23-24.

42. Churchill, *The Grand Alliance*, 424.

43. Sherwood, *Roosevelt and Hopkins*, 318.

44. Ibid., 138.

45. Ibid., 283.

46. Ibid., 321.

47. Letter from Air Vice Marshal David C. McKinley RAF Ret. to the author dated August 14, 1993.

48. Hopkins Microfilm, Reel 19, Flight to Archangel with Mr. Harry Hopkins, July/August 1941, (Hyde Park, N.Y.: Franklin D. Roosevelt Library).

49. Sherwood, *Roosevelt and Hopkins*, 326.

50. Hopkins Collection, *Book 4: Hopkins in Moscow* #6 (Hyde Park, New York: Franklin D. Roosevelt Library).

51. Hopkins Collection, *Book 4: Hopkins in Moscow* #10 (Hyde Park, New York: Franklin D. Roosevelt Library).

52. Ibid.

53. Ibid.

54. Sherwood, *Roosevelt and Hopkins*, 343-44.
55. Nicholas Bethels, *World War II • Time-Life Books: Russia Besieged* (Alexandria, Virginia: Time-Life Books, Inc., 1980), 70.
56. Ibid.
57. Hopkins Collection, *Book 4: Hopkins in Moscow* #10 (Hyde Park, New York: Franklin D. Roosevelt Library).
58. Von Hardesty, *Red Phoenix, the Rise of Soviet Air Power 1941-1945* (Washington, D.C.: Smithsonian Institute Press, 1982), 12.
59. Hopkins Collection, *Book 4: Hopkins in Moscow* #10 (Hyde Park, New York: Franklin D. Roosevelt Library).
60. Ibid.
61. Ibid.
62. Ibid.
63. Sherwood, *Roosevelt and Hopkins*, 330.
64. Hopkins Microfilm, Reel 19.
65. Ibid.
66. Churchill, *The Grand Alliance*, 385.
67. Hopkins Microfilm, Reel 19.
68. Ibid.
69. Churchill, *The Grand Alliance*, 428.
70. Paul Johnson, *A History of the Modern World*, (London: George Weidenfeld and Nicolson Ltd., 1983), 358.
71. Sherwood, *Roosevelt and Hopkins*, 304.
72. Churchill, *The Grand Alliance*, 393.
73. Sherwood, *Roosevelt and Hopkins*, 319.
74. Ibid., 603.
75. Dean Acheson, *Present at the Creation* (New York: W. W. Norton, 1969), 140-41.
76. Winston S. Churchill, *The Hinge of Fate* (Boston: Houghton Mifflin Company, 1950), 392-93.
77. Harold Nicolson, *The War Years 1939-1945* (New York: Atheneum, 1967), 231.
78. Churchill, *The Hinge of Fate*, 401-02.
79. Ibid., 408.
80. Churchill, *The Hinge of Fate*, 266.
81. Winston S. Churchill, *Closing the Ring* (Boston: Houghton Mifflin Company, 1950), 6.
82. Ernest J. King and Walter Muir Whitehill, *Fleet Admiral King: A Naval Record* (London: Eyre and Spottiswoode, 1953), 189-90.

83. Larry I. Bland, ed., *George C. Marshall Interviews and Reminiscences for Forrest C. Pogue* (Lexington, Virginia: George C. Marshall Research Foundation, 1991), 593.

84. Sherwood, *Roosevelt and Hopkins*, 594.

85. Hopkins Collection, *Book 5: Hopkins to London, July 1942* (Hyde Park, New York: Franklin D. Roosevelt Library).

86. Ibid.

87. Ibid.

88. Churchill, *The Hinge of Fate*, 434.

89. Lord Moran, *Churchill Taken From the Diaries of Lord Moran*, 36.

90. Bland, ed., *George C. Marshall Interviews and Reminiscences for Forrest C. Pogue*, 580.

91. Hopkins Collection, *Book 5: Molotov Visit* (Hyde Park, New York: Franklin D. Roosevelt Library).

92. Bland, ed., *George C. Marshall Interviews and Reminiscences for Forrest C. Pogue*, 580.

93. King and Whitehill, *Fleet Admiral King A Naval Record*, 191.

94. Admiral of the Fleet Viscount Cunningham, *A Sailor's Odyssey* (New York: E. P. Dutton, 1951), 465-66.

95. Forrest C. Pogue, *George Marshall, Volume II, Ordeal and Hope 1939-1942* (New York: The Viking Press, 1965), 25.

96. Letter from G. C. Marshall to Mrs. Louise Macy dated July 3, 1942, Marshall Papers, Box 71, Folder 20, George C. Marshall Library, Lexington, Virginia.

97. Sherwood, *Roosevelt and Hopkins*, 607.

98. Arthur Bryant, *The Turn of the Tide* (Garden City, N.J.: Doubleday, 1957), 342.

99. Hopkins Collection, *Book 5: Hopkins To London, July 1942*, (Hyde Park, N.Y.: Franklin D. Roosevelt Library), dated July 1942.

100. King and Whitehill, *Fleet Admiral King A Naval Record*, 193-94.

101. Map Room Collection, Box No. 2, Churchill to Roosevelt, May to July 1942 (Hyde Park, N.Y.: Franklin D. Roosevelt Library), dated June 20, 1942.

102. Bryant, *The Turn of the Tide*, 342.

103. Ibid., 342-43.

104. Ibid., 343.

105. Sherwood, *Roosevelt and Hopkins*, 609.

106. Bryant, *The Turn of the Tide*, 343.

107. John Keegan, *The Second World War* (New York: Penguin Books, 1990), 316.

108. Sherwood, *Roosevelt and Hopkins*, 607.

109. Hopkins Collection, *Book 5: Hopkins to London* (Hyde Park, N.Y.: Franklin D. Roosevelt Library), dated July 1942.

110. Bryant, *The Turn of the Tide*, 343.

111. Ibid.

112. Ibid., 344.

113. King and Whitehill, *Fleet Admiral King A Naval Record*, 197.

114. Ibid, 195.

115. Hopkins Collection, *Book 5: Hopkins to London* (Hyde Park, N.Y.: Franklin D. Roosevelt Library).

116. King and Whitehill, *Fleet Admiral King A Naval Record*, 197.

117. Ibid.

118. Gilbert, *Road to Victory 1941-1945*, 152.

119. Bryant, *The Turn of the Tide*, 346.

120. Ibid.

121. Churchill, *The Hinge of Fate*, 448.

122. Ibid.

123. Keegan, *The Second World War*, 316.

124. Bland, ed., *George C. Marshall Interviews and Reminiscences for Forrest C. Pogue*, 433.

125. Sherwood, *Roosevelt and Hopkins*, Note 612, 954.

126. H. H. Arnold, *Global Mission*, (New York: Harper Brothers, 1949), 323.

127. William D. Leahy, *I Was There* (New York: Whittlesey House, 1950), 111.

128. David McCullough, *Truman* (New York: Simon & Schuster, Inc., 1992), 213.

129. Harry S. Truman, *Memoirs Vol. I: Year of Decisions* (Garden City, New York: Doubleday and Company, Inc., 1955), 31.

130. Truman, *Memoirs Vol. I: Year of Decisions*, 77.

131. Churchill, *Triumph and Tragedy*, 572-73.

132. David Cannadine, ed., *Blood, Toil, Tears and Sweat, The Speeches of Winston Churchill* (Boston: Houghton Mifflin Company, 1989), 303.

133. Truman, *Memoirs Vol I: Year of Decisions*, 258.

134. Sherwood, *Roosevelt and Hopkins*, 774.

135. Allan Bullock, *Hitler and Stalin Parallel Lives* (New York: Random House, Inc., 1993), 894.

136. Churchill, *Triumph and Tragedy*, 365.

137. Bohlen, *Witness to History*, 244.

138. Ibid., 218.

139. Naval Aide Files, Hopkins-Stalin Conference (Independence, Missouri: Harry S. Truman Library), dated May 26-June 6, 1945.

140. Ibid., 4.

141. Ibid., 5.

142. Ibid.

143. Ibid.

144. Ibid., Second Meeting, 2.

145. Ibid., Second Meeting, 8.

146. Ibid.

147. Ibid., Second Meeting, 9.

148. Churchill, *Triumph and Tragedy*, 436.

149. Pavel Sudoplatov and Anatoli Sudoplatov, *Special Tasks* (Boston: Little, Brown and Company, 1994), 477-78.

150. Churchill, *Triumph and Tragedy*, 129.

151. Ibid., 136.

152. Ibid., 145.

153. George F. Kennan, *Memoirs 1925-1950* (Boston: Little, Brown and Company, 1967), 519, 522-23.

154. Ibid., 543.

155. Ibid., 251.

156. Ibid., 212-13.

157. Naval Aide Files, Hopkins-Stalin Fourth Meeting (Independence, Missouri: Harry S. Truman Library), 3-4.

158. Ibid., 5.

159. Naval Aide Files, Navy cable dated May 30, 1945 (Independence, Missouri: Harry S. Truman Library).

160. Naval Aide Files, Hopkins-Stalin, Private Conversations, dated June 1, 1945 (Independence Missouri: Harry S. Truman Library), 2.

161. Naval Aide Files, Hopkins-Stalin Sixth Meeting (Independence, Missouri: Harry S. Truman Library), 4.

162. Lord Halifax, *Fullness of Days* (New York: Dodd, Mead & Company, 1957), 302-04.

163. Sherwood, *Roosevelt and Hopkins*, 870.

164. Bohlen, *Witness to History*, 338.

165. Ibid., 222.

166. Ibid., 243.

167. Sherwood, *Roosevelt and Hopkins*, 930.

168. Ibid., 919.

169. Ibid., 962.

Bibliography

BOOKS

Acheson, Dean. *Present at the Creation.* New York: W. W. Norton, 1969.

Adams, Henry H. *Harry Hopkins. A Biography.* New York: G. P. Putnam's Sons, 1977.

Arnold, H. H. *Global Mission..* New York: Harper and Brothers, 1949.

Bethels, Nicholas. *World War II • Time-Life Books: Russia Besieged.* Alexandria, Virginia: Time-Life Books, Inc., 1980.

Bland, Larry I., ed. *George C. Marshall Interviews and Reminiscences for Forrest C. Pogue.* Lexington, Virginia: George C. Marshall Research Foundation, 1991.

Bohlen, Charles E. *Witness to History.* New York: W. W. Norton and Company, Inc., 1973.

Bryant, Arthur. *The Turn of the Tide.* Garden City, N.Y.: Doubleday and Company, 1957.

Buell, Thomas B. et al. *The West Point Military History Series The Second World War. Europe and the Mediterranean.* Wayne, N.J.: Avery Publishing Group, Inc., 1984.

Bullock, Allan. *Hitler and Stalin Parallel Lives.* London: Harper Collins Publishers, Ltd., 1991.

Churchill, Winston S. *The Grand Alliance.* Boston: Houghton Mifflin Company, 1950.

Churchill, Winston S. *The Hinge of Fate.* Boston: Houghton Mifflin Company, 1950.

Churchill, Winston S. *Closing the Ring.* Boston: Houghton Mifflin Company, 1951.

Churchill, Winston S. *Triumph and Tragedy.* Boston: Houghton Mifflin Company, 1953.

Collier, Peter and David Horowitz. *The Kennedys: An American Drama.* New York: Summit Books, 1984.

Colville, Sir John. *The Fringes of Power.* New York: W. W. Norton and Company, Inc., 1985.

Cunningham, Admiral of the Fleet Viscount. *A Sailor's Odyssey.* New York: E. P. Dutton, 1951.

Dawson, Joseph G. III, ed. *Commanders in Chief Presidential Leadership in Modern Wars*. Lawrence, Kansas: University Press of Kansas, 1993.

Eisenhower, Dwight D. *Crusade in Europe*. Garden City, N.Y.: Doubleday and Company, 1948.

Gilbert, Martin. *Finest Hour Winston S. Churchill 1939-1941*. New York: Heinemann-Minerva, 1989.

Gilbert, Martin. *Winston S. Churchill, Volume VII, Road to Victory*. Boston: Houghton Mifflin Company, 1986.

Halifax, Lord. *Fullness of Days*. New York: Dodd, Mead & Company, 1957.

Hardesty, Von. *Red Phoenix. The Rise of Soviet Air Power 1941-1945*. Washington, D. C.: Smithsonian Institute Press, 1982.

Harriman, W. Averell and Elie Abel. *Special Envoy to Churchill and Stalin 1941-1946*. New York: Random House, 1975.

Hull, Cordell. *The Memoirs of Cordell Hull, Vol. II*. New York: The MacMillan Company, 1948.

Jagerskiold, Stig. *Mannerheim Marshal of Finland*. Minneapolis: University of Minnesota Press, 1986.

Johnson, Paul. *A History of the Modern World*. London: George Weidenfeld Nicolson, Ltd., 1983.

Keegan, John. *The Second World War*. London: Century Hutchinson, Ltd., 1989.

Kennan, George F. *Memoirs 1925-1950*. Boston: Little, Brown and Company, 1967.

Kennedy, Ludovic. *Pursuit*. New York: The Viking Press, 1974.

King, Ernest J. and Walter M. Whitehill. *Fleet Admiral King A Naval Record*. London: Eyre and Spotti‚woode, 1953.

Leahy, William D. *I Was There*. New York: Whittlesey House, 1950.

Lindbergh, Charles A. *The Wartime Journals of Charles A. Lindbergh*. New York: Harcourt Brace Jovanovich, Inc., 1970.

Loewenheim, Francis L., Harold D. Langley and Manfred Jonas, eds. *Roosevelt and Churchill: Their Secret Wartime Correspondence*. New York: Saturday Review Press/E. P. Dutton and Company, 1975.

McCullough, David. *Truman*. New York: Simon and Schuster, 1992.

McJimsey, George. *Harry Hopkins, Ally of the Poor and Defender of Democracy*. Cambridge, Massachusetts: Harvard University Press, 1987.

Moran, Lord. *Churchill Taken from the Diaries of Lord Moran*. Boston: Houghton Mifflin Company, 1966.

Nicolson, Harold. *The War Years 1939-1945 Diaries and Letters.* New York: Atheneum, 1967.

Pogue, Forrest C. *George Marshall, Volume II, Ordeal and Hope 1939-1942,* New York: The Viking Press, 1965.

Schlesinger, Arthur M., Jr. *The Politics of Upheaval.* Boston: Houghton Mifflin Company, 1960.

Sherwood, Robert E. *Roosevelt and Hopkins - An Intimate History.* New York: Harper and Brothers, 1948.

Stevenson, William. *A Man Called Intrepid - The Secret War.* New York: Harcourt Brace Jovanovich, 1976.

Stimson, Henry L. and McGeorge Bundy. *On Active Service in Peace and War.* New York: Harper and Brothers, 1947.

Sturtivant, Ray. *British Naval Aviation the Fleet Air Arm 1917-1990.* Annapolis, Maryland: Naval Institute Press, 1990.

Sudoplatov, Pavel and Anatoli Sudoplatov. *Special Tasks.* Boston: Little, Brown and Company, 1994.

Terraine, John. *The Life and Times of Lord Mountbatten.* New York: Holt, Rinehart and Winston, 1980.

Truman, Harry S. *Memoirs. Vol I: Year of Decisions.* Garden City, New York: Doubleday, 1955.

van der Vat, Dan. *The Atlantic Campaign.* New York: Harper and Row, 1988.

Whitley, M. J. *German Destroyers of World War II.* Annapolis, Maryland: Naval Institute Press, 1991.

Willmott, H. P. *The Great Crusade, A New Complete History of the Second World War.* New York: Macmillan, Inc., 1990.

REFERENCES

Blood, Toil, Tears and Sweat, The Speeches of Winston Churchill. Edited by David Cannadine. Boston: Houghton Mifflin Company, 1989.

The New Encyclopaedia Britannica. Micropaedia, Volume V, 15th ed., 1975, s.v. "Hopkins, Harry Lloyd."

The New Encyclopaedia Britannica. Micropaedia, Volume VI, 15th ed., 1975, s.v. "Mikolajczyk, Stanislaw."

The Times Atlas of the Second World War. Edited by John Keegan. New York: Harper and Row, 1989.

The World Almanac of World War II. First Revised Edition. New York, New York: Pharos Books, 1986.

World War II Airplanes, Volumes I and II. Edited by Angelucci and Matricardi. Chicago: Rand McNally and Company, 1976.

UNPUBLISHED SOURCES

Cable from President Roosevelt to Hopkins, Marshall and King. Hopkins Collection, Box No. 308, Book 5: Hopkins to London, July 1942, #42-3. Hyde Park, New York: Franklin D. Roosevelt Library.

Cable from President Roosevelt to Hopkins, Marshall and King. Hopkins Collection, Box No. 308, Book 5: Hopkins to London, July 1942, #41. Hyde Park, New York: Franklin D. Roosevelt Library.

Cable from Hopkins to President Roosevelt. Hopkins Collection, Box No. 308, Book 5: Hopkins to London, July 1942. Hyde Park, New York: Franklin D. Roosevelt Library.

Conference report from Stalin-Hopkins meeting at the Kremlin, dated July 31, 1941. Hopkins Collection, Book 4: Hopkins in Moscow #10. Hyde Park, New York: Franklin D. Roosevelt Library.

Conference report from Hopkins-Stalin meeting, dated July 30, 1941. Hopkins Collection, Book 4: Hopkins in Moscow #6. Hyde Park, New York: Franklin D. Roosevelt Library.

Correspondence from Air Vice Marshal David C. McKinley, RAF Retired, to the author, dated 26 July 1993; 14 August 1993; 20 September 1993; 17 May 1994 and 23 June 1994.

Engagement book for General George C. Marshall. Marshall Papers, Book 115, Folder 4. Lexington, Virginia: The George C. Marshall Library.

Flight to Archangel with Mr. Harry Hopkins, July/August 1941. Hopkins Microfilm, Reel 19. Hyde Park, New York: Franklin D. Roosevelt Library.

Handwritten memo of Harry L. Hopkins on Claridge's stationery dated January 10, 1941. Harry L. Hopkins Papers, Series III, Box 56, Folder 12. Georgetown University: Special Collections, Lauinger Library.

Interview with Robert Hopkins on May 25, 1993.

Letter dated July 3, 1942, from G. C. Marshall to Mrs. Louise Macy. Marshall Papers, Box 71, Folder 20. Lexington, Virginia: The George C. Marshall Library.

Letter from The Lady Soames, DBE, to the author, dated September 25, 1993.

Memorandum dated June 2, 1942 from Winston S. Churchill to President Roosevelt. Map Room Collection, Box No. 2, Churchill to Roosevelt, May to July 1942. Hyde Park, New York: Franklin D. Roosevelt Library.

Memorandum dated July 16, 1942 from President Roosevelt to Hon. Harry L. Hopkins, General Marshall and Admiral King entitled, "Instructions for London Conference." Hopkins Collection, Box No. 308, Book 5: Hopkins to London, July 1942, #24. Hyde Park, New York: Franklin D. Roosevelt Library.

Memorandum dated May 30, 1942, prepared by S. H. Cross regarding a White House meeting between Roosevelt, Molotov, King, Hopkins, Pavlov and Cross. Hopkins Collection, Box No. 311, Book 5: Molotov Visit. Hyde Park, New York: Franklin D. Roosevelt Library.

Minutes of a Combined Staff Conference held at No. 10 Downing Street, S. W. I. on July 20, 1942. Hopkins Collection, Box No. 308, Book 5: Hopkins to London, July 1942, #40. Hyde Park, New York: Franklin D. Roosevelt Library.

Minutes of a Combined Staff Conference held at No. 10 Downing Street, S. W. I. on July 22, 1942. Hopkins Collection, Box No. 308, Book 5: Hopkins to London, July 1942, #40. Hyde Park, New York: Franklin D. Roosevelt Library.

Navy cable dated May 30, 1945, designated top secret and personal from Hopkins for President Truman. Naval Aide Files, Box 8, Communications File Folder. Independence, Missouri: Harry S. Truman Library.

President Roosevelt's Diaries, Microfiche Collection, Card 12, President's Diaries and Itineraries. Hyde Park, New York: Franklin D. Roosevelt Library.

Record of conversations between Hopkins and Stalin in Moscow May 26 to June 6, 1945. Naval Aide Files. Independence, Missouri: Harry S. Truman Library.

Remarks by Pamela Churchill Harriman at the opening of the private papers of Harry L. Hopkins at Georgetown University on January 26, 1986.

Seating chart for dinner on HMS *Nelson* on January 15, 1941. Harry L. Hopkins Papers. Georgetown University: Special Collections, Lauinger Library.

Index